ENGLISH SILVER
1675—1825

*Christmas, 1980
To Jackie & John Vogelstein
with affectionate regards
Alby Cove(?)
(Arcadia Press)*

ENGLISH SILVER
1675 — 1825

by
Stephen G.C. Ensko
and
Edward Wenham

ARCADIA PRESS

Copyright © 1980, by Abby Goell
All Rights Reserved
Library of Congress Number 80-69593
ISBN: 0-938186-00-0
Printed in the United States of America
0 1 2 3 4 5   6 5 4 3 2 1

PREFACE TO THE REVISED EDITION

Since the original 1937 edition of this book came to our attention, we have found it an indispensable guide to the study of antique silver.

Collecting fine examples of the silversmith's art has long been popular throughout Europe, Great Britain, and in the countries of the Western hemisphere. The sharp rises in the price of the metal itself have focused fresh attention on the intrinsic worth of the material. New collectors and dealers in antique silver, vying for the limited number of desirable pieces, push the price levels higher each year.

The enthusiastic response of buyers, sellers, appraisers, curators and collectors to the news of its republication has reinforced our belief that it offers a unique contribution to the large, often confusing body of literature on the subject. We think it worth republishing for several reasons.

First, over 200 line drawings identify with a precision and clarity far better than photographs, the best work of the time. The changes of style, form, and detail from 1675 to 1825 are presented, as it were, on a silver platter. Each plate will help the reader trace the stylistic development of virtually every type of domestic silver object made in England.

Second, the text is worth reading and rereading. The authors, Messrs. Ensko and Wenham explain, describe, teach, and enlarge upon their subject, all in a clear and organized fashion. The prose is straightforward, precise, but stylish, much like the drawings, with a great deal of specific information in each paragraph.

Third, the format of the book makes it easy to slip into a handbag or coat pocket for a casual browse at auction or market, yet it is complete enough to include all categories of silver in use today. The section on assay marks permits the reader to identify correctly any piece he wishes. The assay marks themselves have been enlarged from the original edition, the punch mark or outline sharpened to allow careful study of the crucial detail.

Fourth, although the book was written by experts who devoted years to its preparation, it is a book with more than a narrow appeal. It is meant for every admirer of English silver who wants to enlarge his understanding. The writer or appraiser who must describe correctly a later copy of a period example will refer to it again and again. The book is free of footnotes, discursive references, and conjecture, keeping to the essential points in each matter. An excellent bibliography, reprinted from the original edition, offers the suggestions and the possibility of pursuing more scholarly and detailed research.

In short, we think *English Silver—1675-1825* is a handbook for everyone interested in this field, to be used and reused, essential for the most basic library in the decorative arts.

ABBY J. GOELL
Arcadia Press

New York, New York
August 1980

FOREWORD

In the preparation of this handbook, an effort has been made to describe, concisely, the changes in style and form that have taken place in English silver during the period 1675 to 1825, and the sources from which those changes sprang. It is, therefore, intended primarily for those whose interest in early silver is directed to the articles which were in daily use by past generations, and which are equally useful in our time.

Line drawings have been employed to insure a more definite outline of form and ornamental details, a knowledge of which is essential in acquiring familiarity with the several variations showing the style in use at a particular period.

Isaac Disraeli, speaking of the relation of the human mind to things antique, refers to the discoveries that can be made in each. As we extend our knowledge, we learn to recognize the skill that is concealed in its form. We find the labor of the craftsman to be as perfect as the metal itself, which, still resisting the moldering touch of time, remains elegant and substantial.

In the study of the various designs and forms, it becomes evident that throughout the ages, many shapes of each period are, more or less, related to those of previous eras, and further, that an appreciable number of them were inspired by natural forms.

Thus, for example, the bowls of some goblets, beakers, straightsided tankards, mugs, coffee-pots and other objects spring from a common origin—the ancient ox-horn cup. The pear-shape which was copied by the silversmiths from the Chinese vase is another. While the outline of this is associated with the pear, it might have derived as well from the ancient Greek lyre, which was first formed of two horns joined. The pear-shape is obviously, more quickly recognized in the Early Georgian undecorated pieces, but it is found in a number of cups made a century or more before. The lower part of the inverted pear-shape, which is shown in several of the illustrations, is quite similar to the bowls of some cups that have survived since the sixteenth century.

Shapes of Cup-bowls were taken from the ostrich-egg, cocoanut, gourd, and other natural forms; the hemispherical shape of the vessels we call bowls are variations of these. Similarly, the first spoon was a shell. In fact, the silversmiths owed most of the ornamental forms to Nature.

For centuries past, English silver styles have been influenced by those of Continental countries, principally France, Germany, and to a lesser extent, Holland. Both the heavy and profuse decoration and many of the shapes of the Tudor and Early Stuart periods were introduced from Germany; the numerous cups and other objects of thin silver decorated with flowers, foliage and animals embossed in high relief, which appeared after the return of Charles II, were copied from the Dutch styles; the chased and pierced work found on some cups, and the effective cut-card work also of the Restoration period, originated in France. The rococo style of the Early Georgian period is also of French origin.

In the latter part of the seventeenth century, there was a pronounced vogue for Oriental shapes and decoration. The silversmiths reproduced the outlines of the Chinese vases and jars with covers, and more or less skillfully engraved their work with figures, flowers and other decorations copied from the painted designs on the porcelain pieces. Similar Chinese decorations were also engraved on cups and tankards, and punch-bowls.

Another style of ornament which made its appearance toward the end of the seventeenth century was spiral convex and concave flutes embossed round the base of such articles, and two-handled cups and porringers with a band of small punched ornaments immediately above.

With the introduction of the higher standard of silver, which is dealt with in the Notes on Silver Marks, there was a very definite change in the style and decoration of silverwork. Simplicity of outline superceded the former elaborate embossed work, such ornamentation as was employed being restricted to certain forms. This restriction was due to the new standard of silver containing less alloy. Alloy, which is generally copper, is added to harden the silver. Consequently with the softer metal, decoration had to be limited to such types as would not be easily damaged, either when the article was in use, or when being cleaned by the often careless hands of servants.

Silver of this period is more generally spoken as of Queen Anne, though, actually, the High Standard period includes the last four years of the previous reign of William III, the whole of Queen Anne's reign, and the first five years of the period of George I. It lasted less than twenty-five years, during which household silver of plain styles was fashionable. There are, however, several ornamental forms, and these demonstrate the ingenuity and skill of the silversmiths in overcoming the restrictions imposed by the softer metal. Some of these forms are largely characteristic of the period, as, for example, the cut-card work which was developed to a remarkable degree, and applied with considerable effect to various objects.

The effective use of this decoration is seen at its best in coffee and chocolate-pots with flat bases, and applied to the lower part of the bowls of ewers, wine-coolers and like shapes. With the coffee and chocolate-pots, elaborate leaf forms, cut from thin silver, are applied to the back of the wooden handle, to the body round the handle sockets, and round the joint of the spout. Even more ambitious cut-card work is applied to the ewers, wine-coolers and similar round-bottom objects, for with these the outline often will be pierced in intricate shapes to suggest a calyx. This is one of the most attractive styles of decoration found at any period.

Other characteristic ornaments employed by the silversmiths during the time the High Standard silver was in force are a large gadroon very frequently used as a border or band, and the short concave flute with rounded ends, chased vertically round the bodies of tankards, mugs and punchbowls.

Though the term "Georgian period" is commonly used to denote, approximately one century (about 1725 to 1830), the fact that two very distinct styles were fashionable during that time makes it advisable and necessary to divide the period into Early Georgian (about 1725 to 1765), and Late Georgian (about 1765 to 1830).

During the first five years of George I's reign, the High Standard silver was still in force, and it was not until some few years after the old sterling standard was restored that the vogue of plain silver finally passed. Then, a few years before the second George came to the throne, the more ornate forms, fashionable in France some years before, which had been introduced to England by the Huguenot silversmiths, became fashionable in London. It is this style which is known as the rococo.

A brief definition of the term "rococo" will to a large extent describe the more outstanding features by which silverwork of that style may be recognized. It implies various ornamentation imitating rockwork, is derived from *roc et coquille* (rock and shell), or from rocaille (rockwork). The rococo style originated in Italy but its later development was brought about by a school of designers in Paris. Its foremost protagonists were Jules-Aurele Meissonnier and Francois Boucher, the former being responsible for the most extravagant designs in the rococo style. Meissonnier was made director of the Royal Factory of Paris, in 1723, and later master of the Guild of Silversmiths. It was the florid designs which he produced that so strongly influenced the celebrated Paul de Lamerie.

Possibly it is due to Lamerie's leadership of the rococo school in England, and the fact that he wandered into the bizarre, that fostered the suggestion that the silversmiths of the rococo period concealed beauty of outline with a mass of superfluous ornamentation. This may apply to isolated objects made by Lamerie, by some of his fellow Huguenots, and his English emulators. Yet it is evident in any representative collection of Early Georgian silver that the silversmiths practised, and their patrons preferred, the less exuberant ornamentation.

No suggestion could be made of lavishness in such mounts as the gadroon and shell, the scroll and shell, the flat chased flowers, scrolls and other motifs often applied to bowls and like articles, or to cartouches within shells, as that shown in the Warwick cruet-frame on page 53.

The restrained use of shell ornaments with candlesticks, the well-balanced scroll branches of candelabra, the pierced work of baskets and epergnes, and the chased work on the shoulder of a tea-pot or tea-kettle are splendid. Whenever one of these decorations is employed, it is invariably appropriate to the object to which it is applied, yet each is characteristic of the rococo style of decoration.

Some few years after George III came to the throne in 1760, English silver underwent a change as radical as that which had occurred about 1725. The change in George III's reign was fundamentally inspired by the discoveries at Herculaneum and Pompeii, though, in England, it was largely stimulated by the architectural designs of Robert and James Adam. These designs were based upon the ancient classic orders. When the Adam brothers extended their activities to interiors, they also designed furniture in keeping with the new fashion. They were responsible, too, for some silver designs which, with the published pictures of the metal objects found at Pompeii, inspired the silver of what is known as the Neo-Classic, or Adam style.

The shapes of larger silver objects of this period are obviously copied from the Greek and Roman vessels brought to light during the excavations. The various ornamental forms are also of classic origin. References are made in the following pages to the illustrated examples which show the dominating shape of the Adam style ancient vase, particularly in such pieces as two-handled cups, tea-urns, coffee-pots, and jugs. If perhaps not as quickly recognized, it is present equally in many others. Candlesticks reveal the ancient classic influence in the columnar shafts and capitals, and in the applied ornaments.

Ornamental forms of the Adam style are fairly numerous. Most frequently used are festoons, rams' heads, wine leaves and grapes as a running scroll, medallions, drapery, rosettes, laurel and acanthus leaves, pendant husks, lions' feet and masks, and engraved and bright-cut decoration.

This brief review of the historical background, and the evolution of shapes and styles in English silverwork has now reached the end of the eighteenth century. The first quarter of the next century finds the influence of the Adam style gradually waning. It was a struggle between the weakening Neo-classic and the virile Empire designs which had appeared in France after Napoleon returned from Egypt in 1798. Eventually the Empire won, but until that time, there was a school of silversmiths—an always dwindling one perhaps—who upheld the earlier traditions. The silverwork of these men reveals not only their loyalty to the Adam styles, but their reliance upon the rococo period ideas, evident in such designs as the sauce-tureens of 1805 and 1815 illustrated. With the passing of this small band of "loyalists" passed that great era in the history of the English silversmith's art.

Contents

Assay Marks	99
Bibliography	14
Changes Within One Century	85
Foreword	7
Notes on Silver Marks	93
Reminders of Past Traditions	87

Bedroom-Candlesticks, Taper-Jacks and Snuffers	74
Candlesticks and Candelabra	70
Casters, Muffineers and Dredgers	48
Center-Pieces and Epergnes	18
Coffee-Pots, Chocolate-Pots, and Jugs	40
Creamers	26
Cream-Pails and Sugar Baskets	28
Cruet-Frames	52
Dish-Rings, Dish-Crosses, and Coasters	60
Entree-Dishes	56
Inkstands	76
Mustard-Pots	50
Pierced Baskets	20
Punch-Bowls and Monteiths	68
Salt Dishes	46
Salvers and Waiters	44
Sauce-Boats	54
Spoons, Forks, and Knives	79
Sugar-Bowls	30
Tankards, Mugs, and Goblets	64
Tea-Caddies	32
Tea-Kettles	36
Tea-Pots	34
Tea-Services	24
Tea-Trays	38
Tea-Urns	22
Tureens	58
Two-Handled Cups	62

Bibliography

CARRINGTON, J. B. AND HUGHES, G. R. — The Plate of the Worshipful Company of Goldsmiths. 1926.

CLAYTON, MICHAEL — The Collector's Dictionary of the Silver and Gold of Great Britain and North America. 1971.

CRIPPS, W. J. — College and Corporation Plate. 1881.
Old English Plate. 9th ed. 1906.
Old English Plate, Ecclesiastical, Decorative, and Domestic; its makers and marks. 1914.

ELLIS, H. D. — A short description of the ancient Silver Plate belonging to the Worshipful Company of Armourers and Brasiers. 1892.

FOSTER, J. E. AND ATKINSON, T. D. — An illustrated catalogue of the Loan Collection of Plate exhibited in the Fitzwilliam Museum (Cambridge), May 1895. 1896.

GARDNER, J. S. — Old Silver-work, chiefly English, from the XVth to the XVIIIth Centuries; a catalogue of the loan collection exhibited at St. James's Court, London, in 1902. With introductory notes. 1903.

JACKSON, C. J. — An illustrated History of English Plate, ecclesiastical and secular. 2 vols. 1911.

JEWITT, L., AND HOPE, W.H.St.J. — The Corporation Plate and Insignia of Office of the Cities and Corporate Towns of England and Wales. 2 vols. 1895.

JONES, E. ALFRED — The Old Royal Plate in the Tower of London. 1908. Illustrated catalogues of the Collection of old Plate of J. Pierpont Morgan, Esquire. 1908.
The Old English Plate of the Emperor of Russia. 1909.
The Old Plate of the Cambridge Colleges. 1910.
Old Silver of Europe and America. 1925.

Bibliography

MOFFAT, H. C. — Old Oxford Plate. 1906.

OMAN, C. C. — English Domestic Silver. 1934.

OXFORD — Catalogue of a Loan Exhibition of Silver Plate belonging to the Colleges of the University of Oxford. 1928.

PHILIPS, P. A. S. — Paul de Lamerie; a study of his life and work. 1935.

SHAW, H., AND MEYRICK, SIR S. R. — Ancient Plate and Furniture from the Colleges of Oxford and the Ashmolean Museum. 1837.

WATTS, W. W. — Old English Silver. 1924.

WENHAM, EDWARD—Domestic Silver of Great Britain and Ireland. 1931.

Works dealing with the assaying and marking of gold and silver in England, and the marks of the goldsmiths and silversmiths are:

CHAFFERS, W. — Hall-marks on Gold and Silver Plate. 9th ed. 1905.

CRIPPS, W. J. — Old English Plate. 9th ed. 1906.

GRIMWADE, ARTHUR C. — London Goldsmiths, 1697-1837 — Their Marks and Their Lives.

HEAL, SIR AMBROSE — The London Goldsmiths, 1200-1800; a record of the names and addresses of the craftsmen, their shop-signs and trade-cards. 1935.

HERBERT, W. — The history of the Twelve great Livery Companies of London. 2 vols. 1836-7.

JACKSON, SIR C. J. — English Goldsmiths and their Marks. 1905.
PRICE, F. G. H. — A handbook of London Bankers, with some account of their predecessors the early Goldsmiths. 1890-1.

PRIDEAUX, SIR W. S. — Memorials of the Goldsmiths' Company. 2 vols. 1896-7.

ENGLISH SILVER
1675-1825

Center-Pieces and Epergnes

These fine table ornaments may be said to continue the tradition of the standing salt; for as, until the late Stuart period, the great salt was a symbol of social prominence, so center-pieces and epergnes were symbols of wealth during the eighteenth century.

Center-pieces differ in style from epergnes, though both are more generally referred to as epergnes; one of each is illustrated on the opposite page. The center-piece, which was introduced in the time of George I is not as tall, and is somewhat more massive; and, like the one shown, quite often fitted with branches and sockets to hold candles as well as small dishes for almonds, sweet-meats, and a large center dish for fruit. Nor is it difficult to imagine the beauty of such a table ornament when the candles are lighted.

When the pierced silver work became fashionable in about 1750, the solid center-piece was replaced by the delicate epergnes which are more often found on present-day dining-tables. In these, the rococo influence is noticeable in the elaborate scroll legs and shell feet, in the scroll brackets supporting the small pierced dishes, and other decorative motifs. The large dish of the center-piece is replaced in the epergne by a pierced boat-shaped basket, and the candle-brackets are omitted.

Some of the very elaborate epergnes have four columns rising from the base, and supporting a pierced canopy which is sometimes shaped like the roof of a pagoda with pendant bells; but as this type is usually about twenty-four inches high, it is rarely suitable to the average dining-table. The use of the pagoda shape and other forms in epergnes indicates the Chinese influence, which is evident in the furniture of the Chippendale period; and the silversmiths doubtless adapted some of the designs published by Chippendale and other cabinet-makers to their own craft.

1735

1765

Pierced Baskets

Like so many other objects of table silver, the pierced baskets of the Georgian period show the refinement and elegance which began to appear in English society during the early part of the eighteenth century. One of the first styles is oval with sides chased and pierced in the form of wicker work; these had a loop handle at each end, instead of the more graceful bale handle of later baskets. A similar basket without handles, probably for holding bread, was in use a century earlier, but very few of these have survived.

In the reign of George II, they developed a remarkable delicacy in the numerous combinations of pierced designs. These combinations vary considerably; in some, the pierced designs will be scrolls alternating with crosses placed diagonally, as in the basket of 1740 illustrated; in others they will be intricately interlaced scrolls, as in the one of 1770, and there are many other geometric forms showing the versatility and skill of the silversmiths. Later baskets, while retaining the same shape and the bale handle, are far less elaborately pierced and for that reason lack some of the decorative qualities of the earlier examples; either style, however, when filled with fruit is an unusually attractive center on a small dining table; or by placing a shallow dish in the bottom of one of them to hold a little water, the basket can be filled with flowers.

During the reign of George II, cake-baskets in the form of a large scallop shell were made, though examples are rare. These are pierced similarly to the baskets with handles, and fitted with an elaborate cast handle, and raised on three dolphin feet.

With the change of fashion in the early nineteenth century, the pierced style gave place to baskets with wire work sides, or decorated with embossed and chased work, with gadroon and scroll and other mounts. These are either oval or oblong, and many give evidence of fine craftmanship.

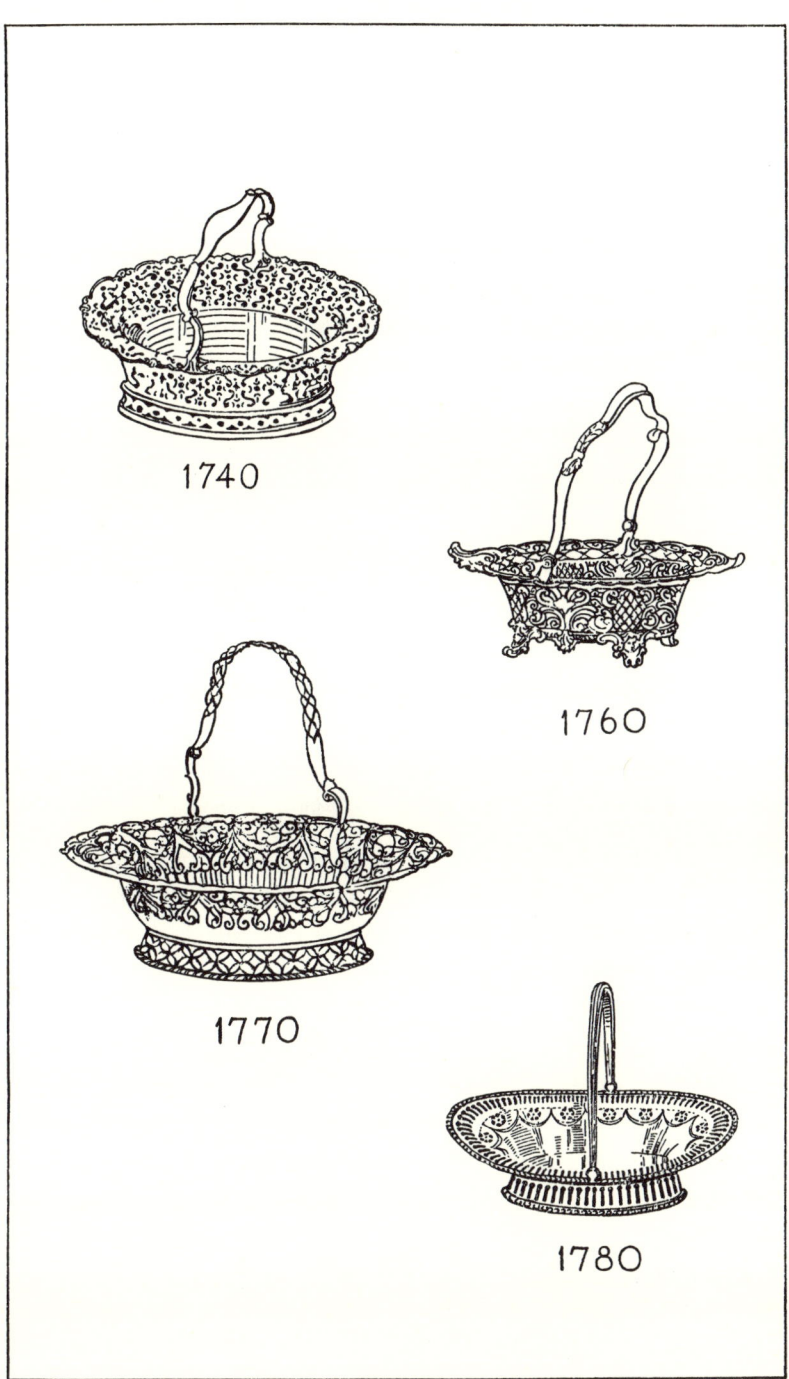

Tea-Urns

It is thought by many that the silver urns fitted with a tap were used before the tea-kettles, but actually the urns did not come into general use until the time of George III. There are various types of these shapely vessels, the earliest having the pear-shaped body either plain or embossed with rococo decoration on an ornamental base with four feet. Probably the most graceful urns are those of the neo-classic period, for these follow the form of the classic vases with two looped handles, as illustrated by those of 1780 and 1785. Traces of the classic influence appear, too, in the urns of the early nineteenth century, but at this time they had become wider and more squatty, and some of the former grace was lost.

When urns were introduced, the tea-kettle went out of fashion to some extent, though it is unlikely that its use was discontinued. Tea was then an expensive commodity and was "brewed" by the hostess in the drawing room; consequently the kettle would be necessary to supply the boiling water. For while water could be boiled in a kettle by the heat of a spirit lamp, to boil the contents of an urn by this means would be a very slow process.

Actually the urns were filled with boiling water for replenishing the tea-pot, or for holding tea which had been made previously probably in earthenware tea-pots, when a larger number were gathered at a tea-party; and though a spirit lamp was sometimes used, the more common method for maintaining the heat in the water was a "box-iron". This is a piece of iron rather like a sash-weight which was made red hot and placed in a socket in the center of the urn. And even, to-day, with all our modern conveniences, when urns are used to hold tea (or coffee) at some large social gathering, this same red hot iron might well be used to advantage, especially for tea, which it will keep hot yet prevent it from "stewing", because the heat in the iron gradually diminishes.

Tea-Services

Although silver "things for the tea table" were made in sets during the first half of the eighteenth century, and tea-pots, cream jugs, sugar bowls, etc., of a similar style might be assembled, any complete services that are to-day readily available date from the reign of George III. There are various styles of tea-services, but those with one of the several types of straight sided tea-pots are possibly the most popular.

Straight-sided tea-pots made of sheet silver became fashionable toward the end of the eighteenth century. They were made circular, oval, or octagonal with flat bases, and were accompanied by a low stand with feet to protect the surface of the table from the heat; the tea-pot of the service at the top of the opposite page is an example. The spouts are straight tapering tubes placed fairly close to the bottom of the side and the handles are either of wood, or of silver insulated with ivory. Some have shaped wavy sides and any applied ornamentation is either bright-cut, or engraved. The accompanying sugar bowl is boat-shaped on a stem with a spreading foot, and fitted with a bale handle, while the cream jug is either the low helmet shape on a flat bottom, or one with a similarly shaped rim, but a conical body on a foot like that of the sugar bowl.

One development from the straight-sided tea-pot is found with the services at the beginning of the last century, two of which are illustrated. In the one of 1800, the tea-pot has a swan-neck spout, and the separate small stand is still used; but with the set of five years later, the stand is superseded by four ball feet. In each case, the coffee pot is conical toward the bottom and is raised on a foot, similar to that of the sugar bowl shown at the top of the page. The cream jug and sugar bowl also follow the curved form of the two larger pieces; and the decoration on each service is restricted to a single engraved band round the rim or body.

Creamers

A Chinese, or anyone who has lived for long in the East will insist that we Occidentals spoil tea by adding sugar and cream, and until the eighteenth century, tea was drunk without these "flavorings." So, as sugar-bowls were not included among household silver until Queen Anne's time, cream-jugs were missing.

Until the vogue for the neo-classic in the late eighteenth century, all the cream-jugs show the influence of the pear-shape. The earliest type is a sturdy little fellow with a bulbous body and a pointed spout raised on a low foot similar to that of the globular tea-pots. A few years later the body is more definitely pear-shape with a shaped rim and wide spout or lip, on three feet; and later still, the body narrows at the bottom in accordance with the undulating pyriform, and the three feet give place to a stem and molded foot, as shown in the one of 1780. The jug of 1760 with the Lion mask feet, also shown, is the style favored by the Irish silversmiths, to which reference is made in the notes on sugar-bowls.

During the Late Georgian period, the pear-shape went out of fashion in favor of the more formal tall conical shape on a stem with square base. Some of these have a light molding applied to the rim but are otherwise plain; others are engraved in a style similar to some of the straight-sided tea-pots. Another somewhat later cream jug is shorter, but the body is larger and has a flat bottom; see the examples of 1785 and 1800.

Cream-jugs seem to have inspired some quite fantastic forms, such as the goat and bee jug, supposedly designed by Nicholas Sprimont who made several of them in silver, while others were made of porcelain when he was manager of the Chelsea works. Then there are the quaint creamers in the form of a cow with its looped tail for a handle to lift it and pour the cream through the open mouth. The "jug" is filled through an opening in the cow's back which has a small hinged cover ornamented with a band of tiny flowers, and a bee in full relief.

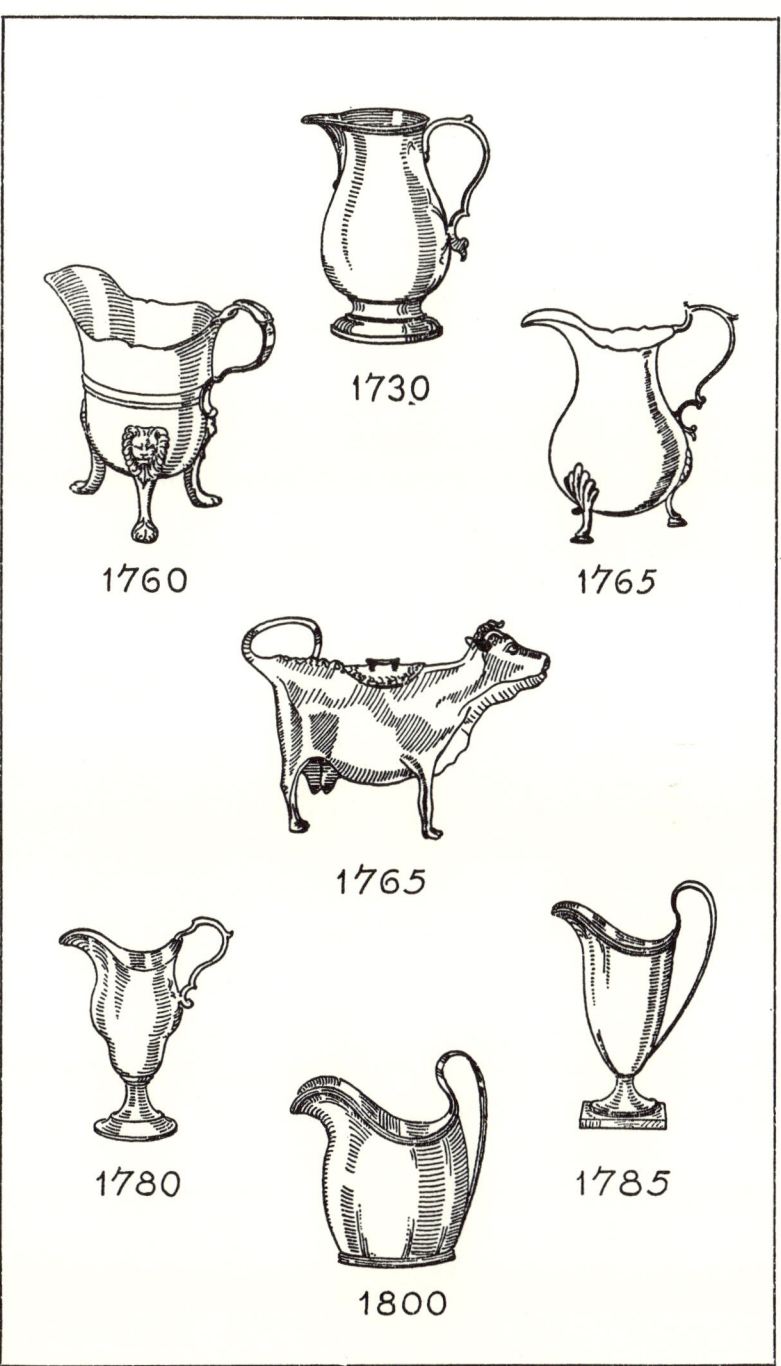

Cream-Pails and Sugar-Baskets

Although pierced silver objects with glass liners (such as the two on the upper half of the opposite page) are more generally described as sugar-baskets, it is a question whether they were not really intended to hold cream. If this is so, then strictly speaking they should be termed cream-pails. The writer has seen similar "pails" used to hold thick cream which was served with a ladle; but this has been not at tea, but at lunch when the cream was eaten with fruit. Irish cream-pails, or piggins, as they are occasionally termed, are chased and pierced in a manner similar to some of the butter dishes (see page 87) and earlier dish-rings, and like the English pail-shaped sugar-baskets were made at the end of the eighteenth century.

The boat-shaped baskets with handles were undoubtedly meant to hold sugar, because the various styles follow those of the straight-sided tea-pots. Some of these baskets are partly pierced, as in the one of 1790, but others are plain or ornamented with engraving, as in that of 1800. The pierced designs vary and in all cases are cut with a precision that is remarkable considering the often minute motifs that are part of the decoration. In many of the pierced forms there is an obvious likeness to those of the cake-baskets; and in some of the tall sugar-vases with covers, the foot is also pierced.

Another method of achieving a pierced design was by means of wire, to which chased leaves and flowers were applied. Sugar-baskets of this type are shaped more like small cake-baskets and are usually earlier than the styles shown on the opposite page; occasionally one is found with spoons, and sugar-nippers to match, in a case with a tea-caddy, but to the average admirer of old silver, they would appeal more as a curiosity than for their beauty.

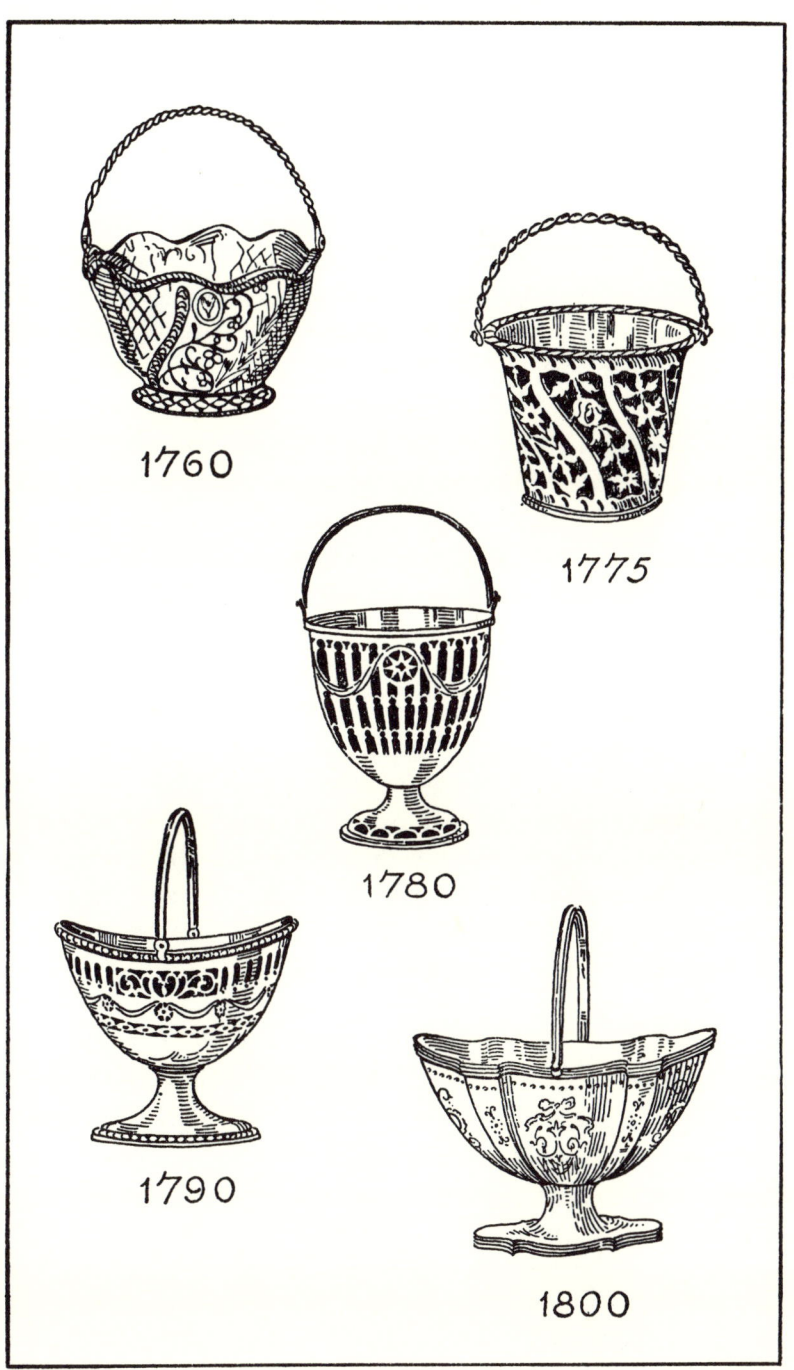

Sugar-Bowls

Judging from such records as exist, the growth of the popularity of tea very considerably increased the consumption of sugar; which doubtless explains why bowls, intended to hold sugar, were first made in the eighteenth century. And that sugar, like tea, was costly is evident from the fact that many of the bowls were fitted with covers; these covers often having a plain or molded ring which allowed it to serve as a stand for the bowl, or as a shallow dish, as shown in two of the bowls illustrated.

While as time went on and sugar became cheaper, this type of bowl was replaced by various uncovered styles, the cover none the less remained more or less popular until well into the nineteenth century. The changes in the shapes are similar to those which, at different periods, appear with the tea and coffee-pots; and the three examples on the opposite page illustrate this, as that of 1735 is obviously related to the globular tea-pots, while the other two have the inverted pear-shape, referred to in connection with other articles of household silver.

During the Late Georgian period hexagonal basins with covers on a low foot ornamented with engraving and bright-cut similar to the tea-pots were fashionable for a time, as were the bowls of classic vase shape with pierced sides and a blue glass liner, of which mention is made with the tea-caddies.

One style which is still widely popular is the typically Irish bowl on three feet. Some of these are fairly plain except for a series of ribs chased from the outside to strengthen the sides, when the rim is either cut in a series of curved forms, or ornamented with a simple mount; others are chased with flowers, fruit and birds when the rim is generally shaped or punched with a row of beads. The Irish silversmiths also made some attractive cream-jugs on three feet to match the sugar basins, but the jugs are not so easy to find.

Tea-Caddies

These formerly essential accessories to the ceremonial of tea-drinking belong to the days when tea was beyond the reach of the modest purse. Though more generally known by the name of "caddy" (from the Malay *kati* meaning a weight equal to 1-1/3 lb., and denoting the small box in which tea was sent to England), the silver boxes for tea were formerly called canisters.

They came into fairly general use concurrently with the silver tea-pot, and some of the first caddies were pear-shape. The type more commonly found dating from the early part of the eighteenth century is bottle-shape with a short neck and slip-on cover, such as the one of 1720 illustrated. Most of the first tea caddies are quite plain, though like other family silver a number of them are engraved with armorial bearings, as is the case with the rectangular one of 1725 and the interesting bottle-shaped example of 1750; but there are many of the rococo period which are elaborately ornamented with scroll-work, flowers, and figures, often in a quite fantastic fashion.

Actually some of these small pieces represent the most skilled craftsmanship both in the shapes and in the ambitious ornamentation; and for that reason they have always attracted the notice of collectors, even though they are rarely used to hold tea in our time. They were also made in sets of three, which are still to be found with the original cases in which they were kept, some of the cases being made of tortoise-shell, or ivory.

In the late Georgian period, many caddies resemble the shapes of the various straight-sided tea-pots and are engraved to match the tea-services of which they were part (two are shown on the opposite page). The vase shape with loop handles was another favorite shape of that time, and these were occasionally accompanied by a similar vase for sugar.

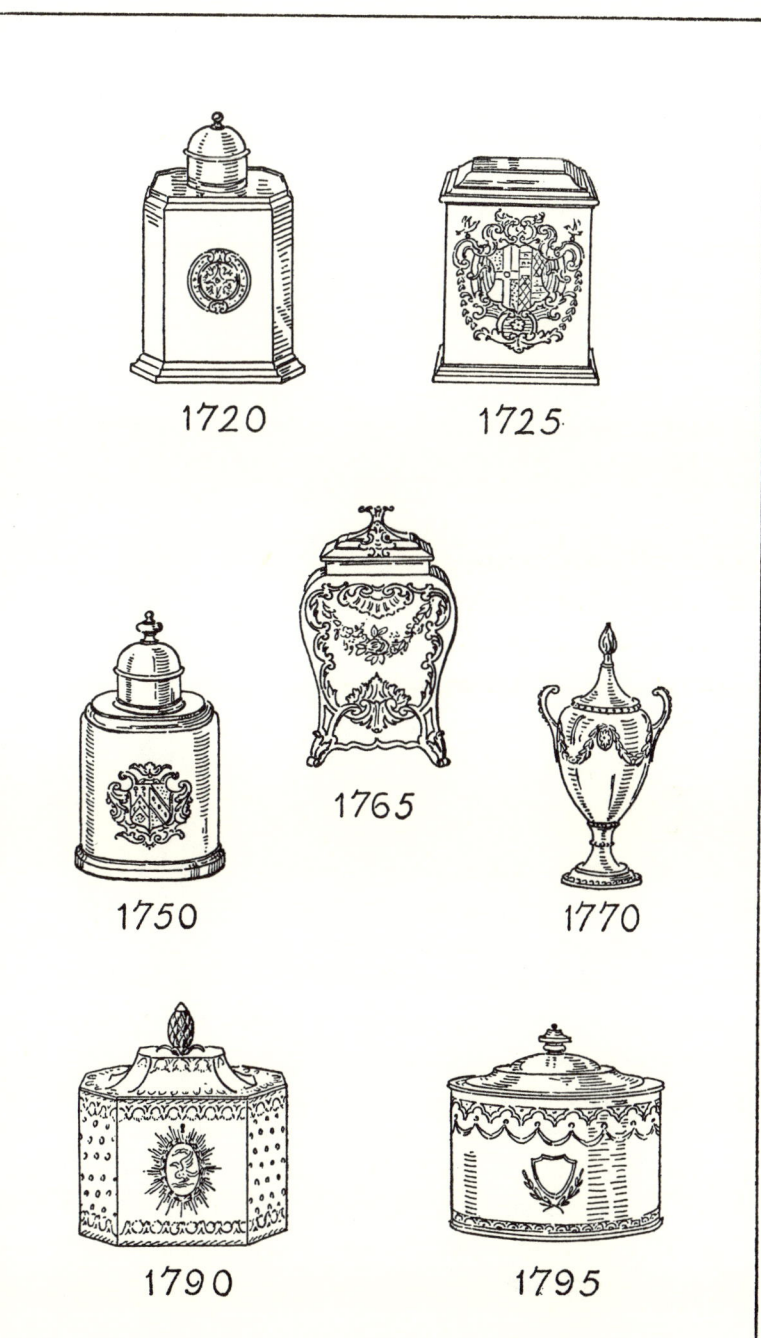

Tea-Pots

It is almost true to say that no eighteenth-century silver teapot is without beauty; admittedly there are a few "freaks" but fortunately they are rare. The reason for this beauty is the fact that the fine curves of the shapes are unspoiled by unnecessary decoration. The early pear-shape with a high domical lid and duck-neck spout is invariably quite plain, the only variation being the octagonal form illustrated by the tea-pot of 1725.

Another type which, like the pear-shape, is as popular today as ever, has the globular body and the straight tapering, or the duck-neck spout. There are several varieties of this type: one has a slightly depressed top with a flush lid and a low ring foot, as shown by the tea-pot of 1720; another, which seems to have been made only by the Scottish silversmiths, is a complete globe, with the lid forming the upper part of the circle — these usually have a rather more elaborate handle of silver, and are sometimes engraved on the shoulder, as in the one of 1735; and another form resembles a slightly flattened globe on a moulded foot, and with this the earlier straight spout is replaced by one with a tendency toward the duck-neck shape, as in the one of 1740.

Some years later the pear-shape was revived but now the wide part of the pear became the top, a "slice" of which was cut off and a high domical lid with a finial fitted. This type, known as the undulating pyriform, is raised on a low stem with a spreading foot, and the handle is usually of wood and the spout is duck-neck shaped, as shown in the tea-pot of 1760. Both the tea-pots at the bottom of the opposite page belong to the late eighteenth century type made of sheet silver with straight sides and flat bottoms, mentioned with tea services. That of 1775 is cylindrical and a trifle deeper than the oval and other shapes; that of 1785 shows the use of the simple but attractive bead mount round the rim and base.

Tea-Kettles

As might be expected, although much larger, tea-kettles at different periods follow closely the shapes of the tea-pot in vogue at the time. When complete, a kettle is accompanied by a stand with a spirit lamp; the earlier stands are tripod but the later ones have four legs. In most cases, the kettle is made to lift off, but some are hinged in front to the stand so that the kettle can be tilted; this arrangement is generally found with the inverted pear-shape, owing to the upper part being much larger than the lower. Where the hinges are used there is a movable pin at the back to hold the kettle firmly on the stand — this can be seen in the illustrations of the kettles of 1750 and 1810.

Comparison with the tea-pots illustrated on the preceding page will show that the shapes are repeated in the contemporary kettles. A few slight variations may be noticed, as for example, in some of the spouts. The more ornamental spouts and the decoration around the shoulders of the kettle of 1750 are also found with tea-pots, and these indicate the rococo influence introduced by the Huguenot silversmiths.

Although the urns for a time replaced the kettles, the latter seem to have been revived when silver services became fashionable, for complete services generally include a kettle on stand en suite with the other pieces. The fluted kettle of 1800 with the engraved band round the rim is one of the several types made of sheet silver, and that of 1810 is one of the shapes evolved during the early nineteenth century from the neo-classic designs. It may be noticed that each of the last three kettle stands has four cabriole shaped supports with claw feet, instead of the tripod of earlier examples; but when the two styles of stands are compared, it is plain that the late Georgian cabriole is merely a modification of the more elaborate scroll.

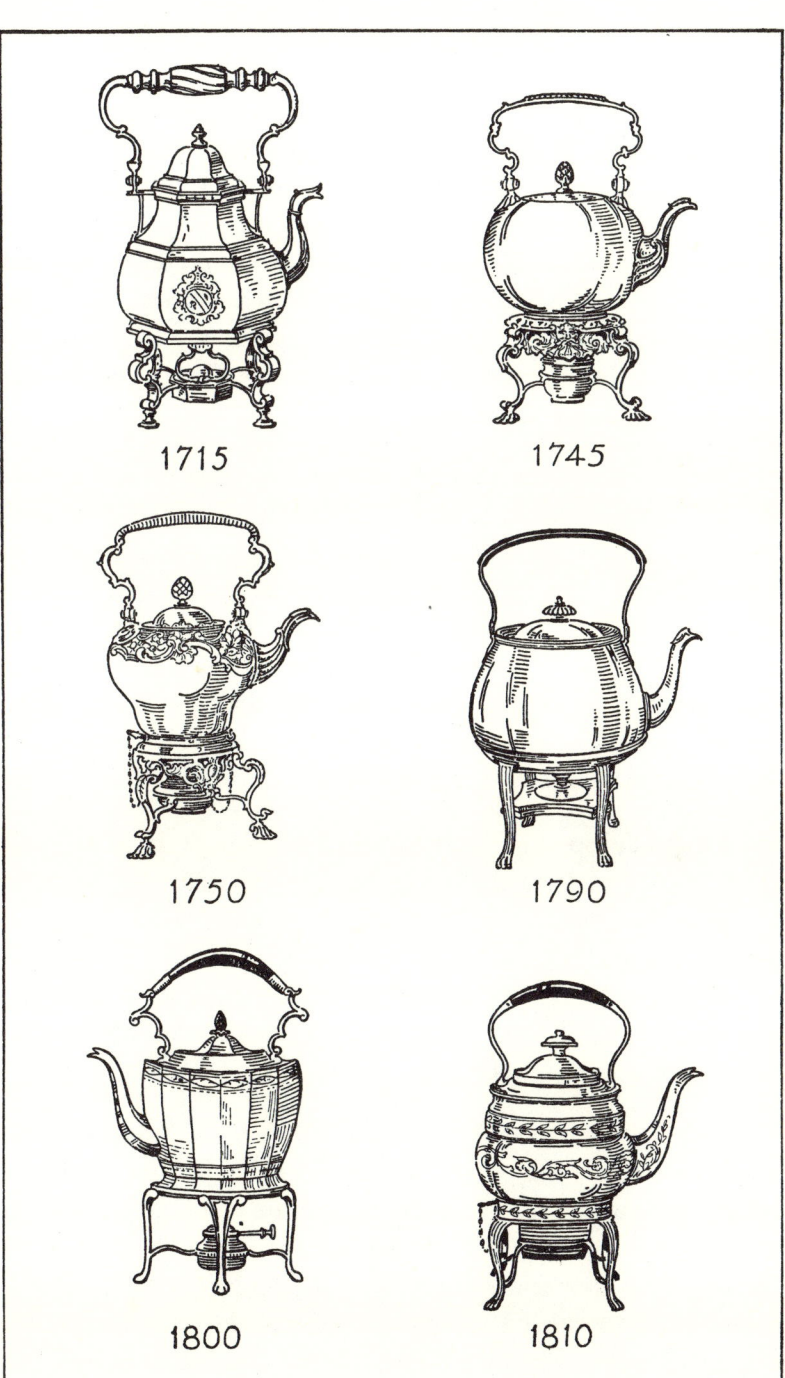

Tea-Trays

Like a number of other articles among eighteenth century household silver, trays are directly traceable to the social custom of drinking afternoon tea. The earlier oblong style has a plain molded edge and incurved corners similar to the salvers, and simplicity of ornament seems to have been preferred by the hostesses of the eighteenth and nineteenth centuries; for while there are trays with more elaborate mounts, thread, reed and ribbon, small bead, gadroon, or other unostentatious mounts are noticeably more prevalent.

Nearly all the later Georgian trays are fitted with a handle at each end for carrying, and the importance of the tea-tray is evident from the fact that mahogany stands were made solely to support them. The tops of these stands were the same size and shape as the silver tea-trays intended for them, and sockets were let into the wood to accommodate the feet of the tray and hold it firmly on the stand. Apparently, too, the silver trays were called "tables", as there are references in early Georgian records to "stands to set the silver Tea and Coffee Tables on."

Generally speaking the surface of tea-trays is quite plain again, except where a coat of arms, or other armorial decoration is engraved in the center; and even where the edges have slightly heavier mounts than those illustrated, this ornamentation is rarely out of proportion to the size of the tray, the gadroon and shell, thread and leaf, and the bead and rosette each being appropriate to an average sized oblong, or oval tea and coffee-tray.

One style of tray which came into fashion during the late Georgian period, but which is rarely seen today has a pierced gallery with hand-holes at each end, but this type does not seem to have had any particular vogue, though it may be said in its favour that it is especially useful for carrying wine glasses. Sometimes, too, the pierced vertical galleries were fitted to an oval bottom of mahogany inlaid with lighter colored wood.

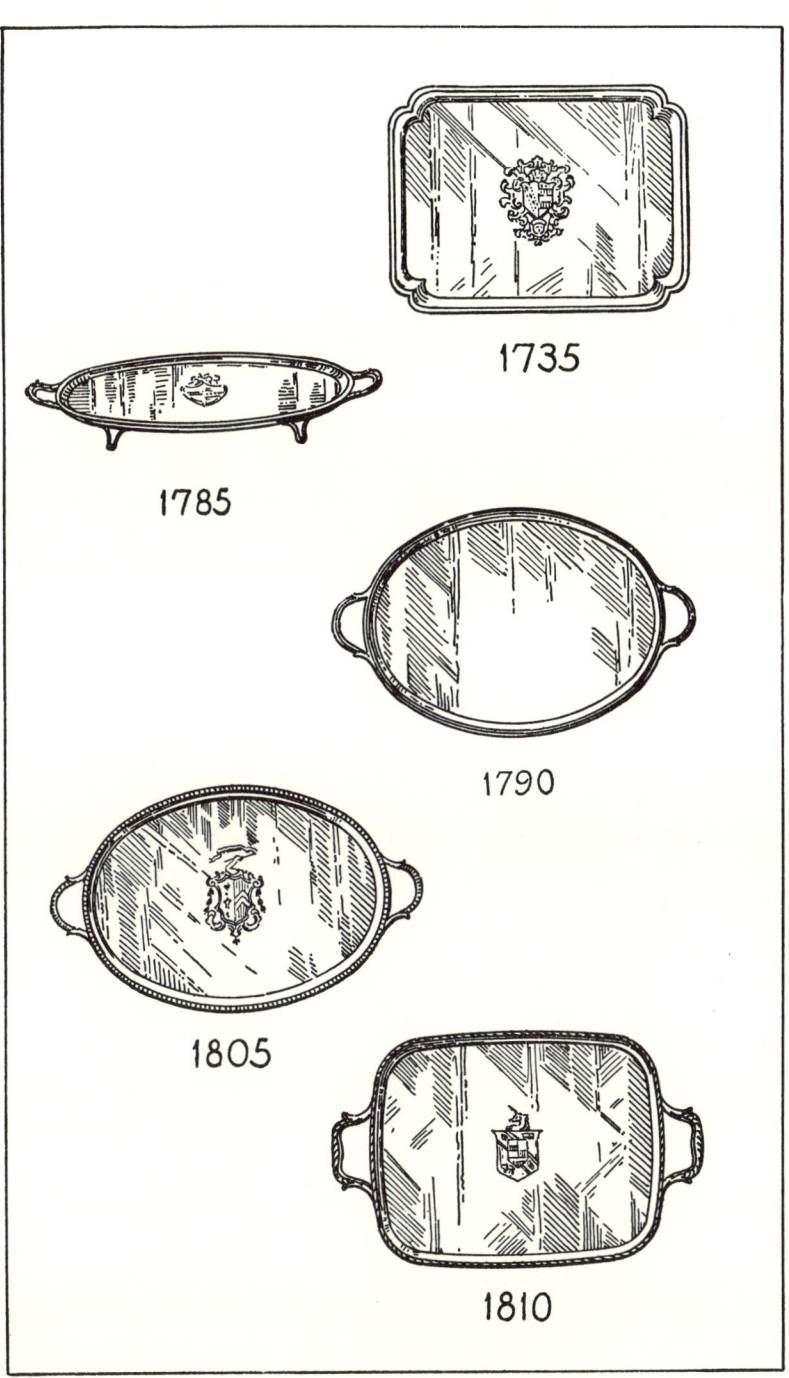

Coffee Pots, Chocolate Pots, and Jugs

When coffee, chocolate and tea were first known in England, the silver pots used were a rather crude tall tapering cylinder with a plain tubular spout and a high cone-shaped cover. The tea-pot of this type disappeared, however, when copies were made from the Chinese porcelain tea-pots, but both the coffee and chocolate-pots kept the tall form. And those with the straight tapering body and flat bottom of the Queen Anne and early Georgian periods closely resemble the first silver pots, though, obviously, with certain refinements such as swan-neck spouts, and the finely shaped domical covers. Another variation in the tall straight-sided coffee and chocolate-pots was the octagonal form with a somewhat heavier moulding round the flat base, as in the one of 1720, illustrated, and the one on the stand with a spirit lamp, illustrated on page 43, the latter having the handle at a right angle with the spout.

The shape of the graceful pear-shaped pots might be said to have been a gradual evolution. The first sign of it occurs in the rounding of the bottom with only a slight suggestion of an incurve to the straight sides; and with the coming of this change, the earlier flat bottom is replaced by a low molded foot as shown in the example of 1745. Within a few years the full pear-shape is adopted, and restricted ornamentation is introduced, such as the more elaborate spout, and the bead, or gadroon band round the rim and foot.

When the neo-classic or Adam style of the last quarter of the eighteenth century became fashionable, the former graceful coffee and chocolate-pots were replaced by the shapes copied from the classic vases. These are embossed and chased with festoons, acanthus leaves, flutes and similar classic decorations, but they lack the attraction of the plain outlines of the earlier straight-sided and pear-shapes.

Early chocolate-pots are in every way similar to those used for coffee, but some of them can be distinguished by a small covered hole in the lid through which a wood swizzle-stick was

COFFEE-POTS, CHOCOLATE-POTS AND JUGS

inserted to stir the chocolate and prevent its settling at the bottom. Later chocolate-pots so closely resemble the jugs used for hot water, that it is difficult to decide which were intended for chocolate and which for hot water or hot milk.

Jugs with lips, such as the octagonal pear-shaped example of 1710, and the plain pear-shape, today, find many uses even if chocolate is no longer fashionable; their more common present day uses are for hot water to replenish the tea-pot, and for hot milk.

Some of the pear-shaped tea-pots are equipped with a tripod stand and spirit lamp, as that of 1710. In view of the unpleasant taste of tea when it is "stewed", it is difficult to understand quite why the lamp was necessary; unless the same pot was used also for coffee — which is the use these rare pots and stands are often put to nowadays. Virtually no change was made in the spirit lamp and stand since it was first introduced, as may be seen by comparing the one with the plain jug of 1800 and the earlier examples shown on the same page.

The less familiar vessel of 1785, illustrated, is known as an argyle which was introduced in about 1780 for holding hot gravy; but, nowadays, they are more generally used for hot milk, coffee, and sometimes, for tea, when only a small quantity is needed. There are several types and each is ingenious, for they are fitted with an inner container, to which the spout is connected, and there is consequently a space between the container and the outside wall of the vessel. By pouring boiling water into an orifice — the one illustrated has a hinged lip at the back through which the water is poured — the gravy (or coffee, or milk) in the inner section is kept hot. Others have a hot-water container in the base.

Salvers and Waiters

Actually the strict distinction between a salver and a waiter has yet to be defined; perhaps no difference exists, for the word salver comes from the Spanish *salva* meaning the tasting of foods before they were served — the "samples" being handed to a guest on a plate, or small tray; and the word waiter, from the Old French, *waitier,* (to attend upon, or watch).

Small early salvers on feet really replaced the former tazza on a foot on which a glass of wine is served. The first salver is square with the corners incurved and the edges of the depressed surface either plain or finely engraved, as illustrated in the example of 1730. Others of about the same time are circular with shaped edges and plain molded mounts; one of which is known as the Chippendale mount, because of its similarity to the carved edges of some Chippendale tea tables, as may be seen in the third salver on the opposite page. Another mount that appeared later is the shell and scroll illustrated in the example of 1755; while that of 1770 has a simpler molded edge with a beaded border. Though ornamental engraving was applied to some salvers, most of them are quite plain except for an engraved coat of arms; and even when engraved decoration is used it is restricted.

As with other silver of the Late Georgian period, the effect of Robert Adam's neo-classic designs is seen in the ornamentation of salvers, the distinguishing features of that time being various classic forms chased on the borders, which in some instances are pierced.

The quite small salvers, generally referred to as card trays, were probably at one time used as stands for tankards and pots, and they too are therefore a descendant of the earlier salvers on a stem with a spreading foot, which are mentioned by a seventeenth-century writer as, "A new fashioned piece of plate broad and flat with a foot underneath and is used in giving Beer or other liquid thing to save the Carpit or Cloathes from drops".

Salt Dishes

When in these prosaic times, you are placed to the right of your host at dinner, you are enjoying the social distinction of being "nearest the salt"; for in the days when the massive salt, some of which were sixteen inches in height, signified the "high" table, this symbol of social prominence was placed a little to the right of the master of the house.

There were other smaller salt-cellars on the table, and from these salt was taken on the end of the knife to the trenchers, which explains their being known as trencher salts. Some few rare trencher salts of the late seventeenth century, of which one is shown here, are taller, and to some extent represent a lingering relic of the earlier standing salts; but the trencher salt proper is a delightfully simple piece of table silver, as is evident in the example of 1725, which is octagonal with incurved sides and plain moldings.

During the Early Georgian period, the circular bowl on three, and sometimes four, feet came into fashion. Some of these are quite plain with perhaps a molded or a gadroon rim; and in some the bowl is chased with floral or other decoration. Another type was a small hemispherical bowl on a molded spreading foot, the bowl occasionally being ornamented with applied leaf motifs.

This circular style became more or less unfashionable when the Adam designs were introduced, and was replaced by a variety of quite attractive salt-cellars, of which four types are illustrated. The one of 1775 has a pierced oval body fitted with a blue glass liner, on four lion-claw feet; these occasionally have claw and ball feet similar to those of the Early Georgian and Chippendale furniture. The one of 1780 is also oval, but it is more boat-shaped, and the decoration is confined to a band of acanthus leaves. The graceful boat-shape, with or without handles, is another Late Georgian salt-cellar that was made in fairly large numbers. These are, with few exceptions, undecorated, any ornamentation being restricted to a simple mount such as the bead round the rim and foot of the example of 1785 illustrated.

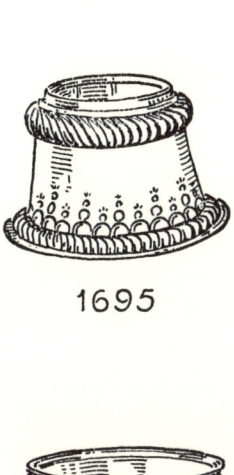
1695

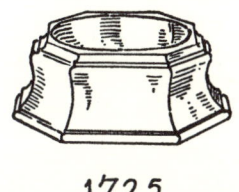
1725

1745

1775

1780

1785

1790

Casters, Muffineers, and Dredgers

Here again, we have different names which to all intents and purposes denote the same article. The more generally used to signify the various small containers with pierced tops is caster; each of the others is of ancient origin, muffineer, strictly speaking, being a small caster used to sprinkle salt, spices, or other flavouring on muffins, while the name dredger probably comes from "dredge" which was a sweetmeat containing spices. Perhaps, therefore, it will be more advisable here to refer to them all as casters.

From those illustrated, it is obvious that the variation and changes in the shapes followed those found with other table silver during the eighteenth century. The cylindrical shape with the gadroon band round the base and top of the 1700 example had appeared some years before; the two small projecting "ears" indicate that the top is fastened to the body by a bayonet joint. This ingenious and efficient fastening is achieved by the two ears, or lugs, being fixed to the lower part of the pierced top; these lugs pass two notches in a grooved molding round the rim of the lower section, and by a slight turn fasten the top firmly to the body.

Small cylindrical, or octagonal casters with a simple scroll handle were also made during the first part of the eighteenth century, and delightful little pieces they are. But the most prevalent is the pear-shape which was copied from the Chinese porcelain vases. Most of these have tall covers, delicately pierced with various forms, but occasionally one will have a quite low domical cover as in the caster of 1730.

With the exception of those having the undulating pyriform (illustrated in the 1760 example) the lower part is hemispherical, the curves of the upper section of the bodies vary, and a number of them are octagonal in form. Toward the end of the eighteenth century, quite small casters were made with pierced sides and fitted with glass liners, but these cannot be regarded as of any importance.

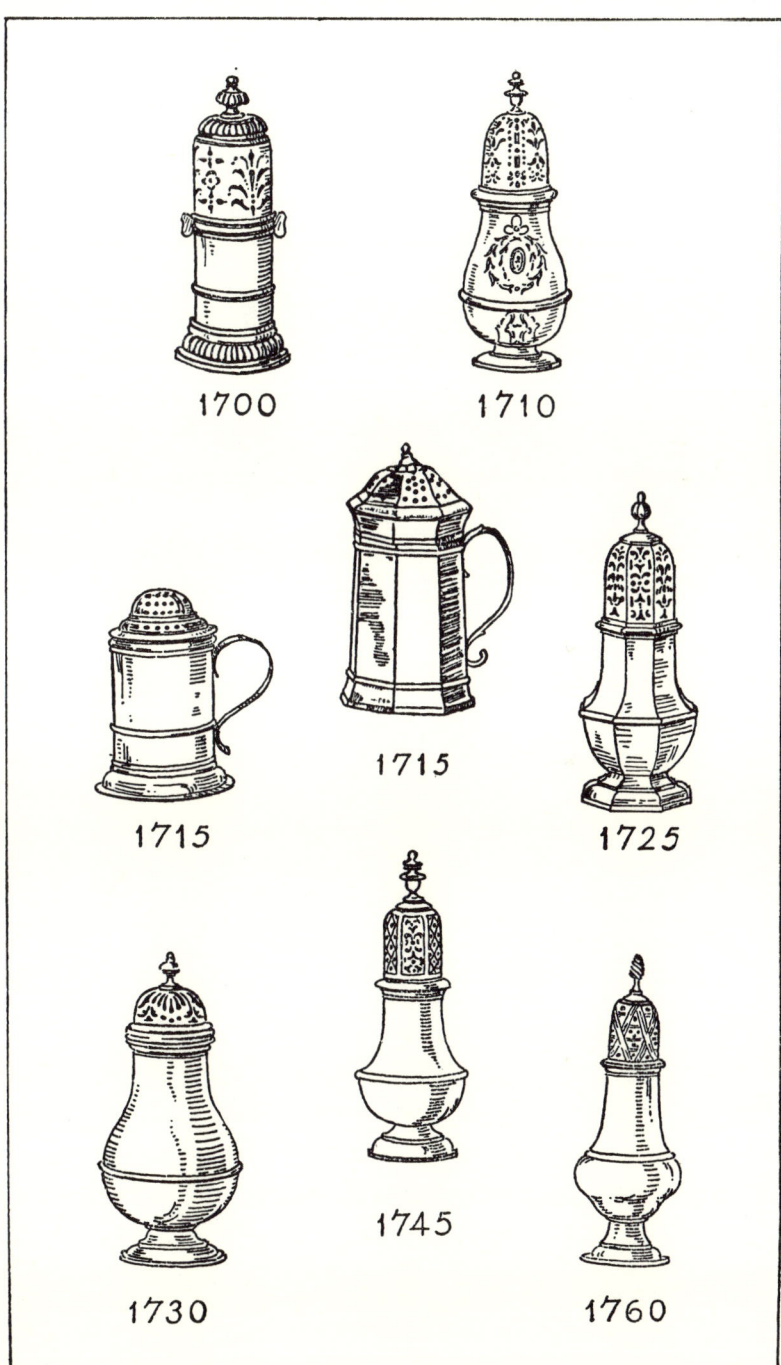

Mustard-Pots

Although mustard was doubtless known for adding piquancy to the roast beef of England several centuries ago, it was then served in earthenware pots with bone spoons. Silver mustard-pots were made in the time of Charles II, but it is unlikely they were in general use until the time of George III.

After they became fashionable the variety of shapes and styles which were produced are even more numerous than those of salt-cellars and pepper-casters. By far the larger number are round or oval; the reason for this was probably due to these shapes being more easily cleaned of the mustard which has a tendency to cling. It also discolors silver when it comes in contact with it, which makes it advisable that even the mustard pots with plain sides should be fitted with a glass liner.

Liners are obviously necessary to those with pierced sides, which was the method of decorating a considerable number of them, and the piercing varies to a remarkable degree. One of the favourite designs before the Adam styles became really fashionable, was the geometric arrangement shown in the mustard pot of 1765, but the later ones are far more ambitious. Urns have the background cut away and narrow pierced bands round the body, floral designs and classic foliage, vertical bars (pales) with two intersecting bands, running scrolls, and numerous other motifs which are brought into attractive relief by the deep blue of the glass liner.

During the early part of the nineteenth century, the pierced styles were gradually discarded and plain sides became popular. A number made at this time are rather like miniature drum-shaped tankards, as is illustrated by the mustard pot of 1810 which has a body and cover quite similar to some tankards of the Late Stuart period.

Cruet-Frames

It is rarely, nowadays, that a cruet-frame is seen on a dining-table except in houses where the earlier customs are still observed; yet most of them represent remarkably fine silverwork. Incidently, the word "cruet" applies only to the glass bottles, and has come down from medieval times when glass bottles were used to hold various flavorings.

Important cruet-frames of the Early Georgian period are fitted with one large and two small silver casters, in addition to the glass bottles which have silver neck-bands and spouts and, generally, silver handles. The large caster was used to hold sugar, and the two smaller ones, Jamaica and Cayenne pepper; and some of the fine sets of three casters which are offered at rare intervals were doubtless made originally for a cruet-frame.

Two Early Georgian frames are shown on the opposite page. The one of 1730 has the skeleton frame, and the casters and the glass bottles are octagonal. That of 1750, which is the style referred to as the Warwick frame, has a base plate of cinquefoil shape on three scroll supports with shell-shaped feet, and a handle on a central rod. Another feature of the Warwick frame is the cartouche enclosed in rococo scrolls, for the coat of arms. With some of these frames, the glass bottles have silver caps, in which instances two small rings are attached to the frame to hold the silver caps when the bottles are in use.

While Late Georgian cruet-frames are equipped with splendid glass bottles, silver casters are no longer among them. The frames are either pierced as shown in the one of 1790, or decorated with engraving. Another popular and smaller cruet-frame of that period has a boat-shaped base on feet, either with a handle at each end, or a central handle. This type enjoyed considerable popularity, because of its smaller size and more elegant form.

1730

1750

1790

1810

Sauce-Boats

In the word "boat" as applied to these graceful little vessels is the survival of an ancient origin, now almost forgotten. The sauce-boats with which we are more generally familiar, while showing some trace of the earlier shape, actually have but a remote likeness to the outline of a boat; but the first type of which examples dating from the first part of the eighteenth century are still in use, resemble the hull of an ancient ship. These rarer sauce boats have a lip at each end, and are fitted either with a bale handle, or a small scroll handle at each side, as is the case with the example of 1725 illustrated.

Within a few years, however, this style was discarded in favor of the slightly smaller sauce-boat with one wide lip and a scroll handle. The first of this more convenient type has a molded spreading foot similar to that of the double-end boats, but this soon gave way to the more attractive three feet. A variety of feet were used, but the most favoured were the hoof and the shell. The shell indicates the rococo influence introduced by the Huguenot silversmiths from France, and this same ornament is generally repeated at the joint of the legs to the body of the sauce-boat, as in the two at the bottom of the opposite page.

Occasionally, a lion mask is used in place of the shell ornament; and it is interesting to notice in this the relationship between the silver and furniture designs, for the lion mask is often found on the legs of chairs and tables of the Early Georgian period. The edges of the Early Georgian sauce-boats — excepting the fantastic conceptions of the extreme rococo style — are usually shaped in a series of cyma curves without mounts, but later a mount was applied to the rim more usually the gadroon, as shown in the one of 1760.

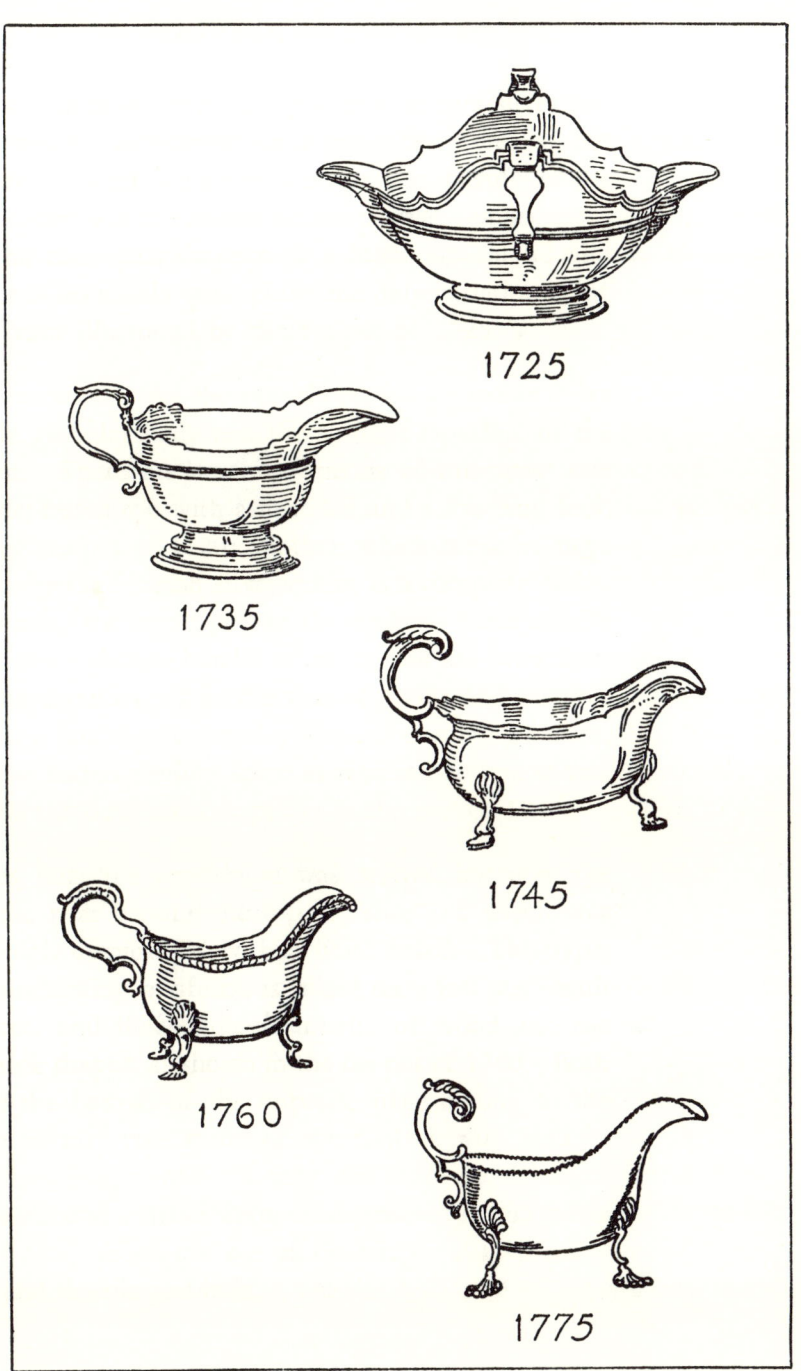

Entree-Dishes

Silver has from past ages been the symbol of wealth; and this is especially the case during the later Georgian days, when the increasing prosperity finds expression in the large silver dinner services. Each of these services included a number of entrée dishes, and when they have been dispersed, the entrée-dishes have often become separated from the rest of the service; because while few families today use a complete silver dinner service, silver entrée-dishes are as fashionable now as two centuries ago.

After entrée-dishes came into use, various shapes were produced by the silversmiths, and various conveniences were added to them. Some of the larger ones are round with a movable division for different vegetables, but the more usual shapes are oblong, oval, or octagonal. In many instances, the cover is made with a flat top and fitted with a detachable handle, so that, when required, the cover can be used as an additional dish; in some of the octagonal shape, the cover is without the usual handle in the centre, but is fitted with one at each end, as illustrated in the dish of 1805.

Another type of cover-dish is slightly shallower as that of 1775; these were probably intended originally for breakfast use and were placed on the warmer on the sideboard. Some of the entrée dishes are fitted in a separate base on feet in which boiling water is placed to keep the heat in the food; and one type of cover-dish, often used for savouries (of which one is shown) has a long turned wood handle; this handle screws into a socket which serves as an orifice through which hot water is poured into a compartment below the dish proper. While important objects of silver, entrée-dishes are never ornate, any decoration being restricted to a mount round the top and edge of the cover. This may be a gadroon, a reed, a bead or other equally simple form.

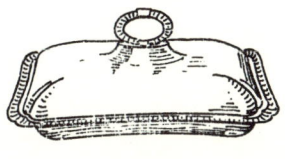
1775

1785

1790

1795

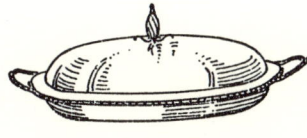
1800

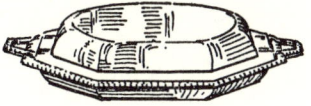
1805

1815

Tureens

As a rule, the various styles are quite simple, though restrained decoration is added to some of the tureens, as in the case of the one of 1760, shown on the opposite page. This indicates the rococo influence, the bowl being ornamented with applied scrolls where the claw feet join the body, and the gadroon at the edge of the cover takes a scroll form, while the cover itself is ornamented with foliage and a floral finial knob. When in use the tureens are placed on a silver dish, and some of them have a dish fixed to the foot; the latter method, however, never became popular as it causes considerable difficulty in cleaning.

This same outline and general treatment occurs again in tureens of the early nineteenth century after the passing of the neo-classic vogue; this is illustrated in the example of 1815 which, if not so elaborate, has similar claw feet with applied leaf decoration above, and the gadroon mount on the edge of the cover.

It is said, and not without reason, that no tureen surpasses the grace of the boat-shape with the angular, or plain loop handles which were fashionable during the neo-classic, or Adam period of the late eighteenth century. These are perhaps the more attractive for the reason that there is no applied decoration to interrupt the rhythm of the curves. This style is invariably supported on a low foot with an oval, or square base, and, apart from the gadroon mount and perhaps some delicately chased leaves or other unobtrusive decoration on the cover, they are quite plain.

Sauce-tureens are smaller copies of the imposing vessels from which soup was ladled into the plates at the sideboard. They were used to hold sauces or gravy used throughout various courses of the dinner.

1760

1785

1805

1815

Dish-Rings, Dish-Crosses, and Coasters

Anyone with Irish antecedents becomes emphatic in his explanation of what a dish-ring is whenever he hears it called by the quite ridiculous name "potato-ring". He would tell you that, at one time, a dish-ring remained in the center of the table throughout dinner to serve as a decorative stand for various bowls as they were brought to the table, namely, the soup, potato (this was usually of bog-oak with or without a silver rim), dessert, and, on occasion, the punch bowl.

Irish dish-rings were made during the last half of the eighteenth and early nineteenth centuries. There are three distinct varieties: the earliest are quite shallow, often less than 5 inches, and show the rococo influence in the pierced scrolls and other motifs; those of the middle period are slightly deeper, chased and pierced with pastoral scenes and figures; and those of the third are pierced in the Adam style with vertical pales, chased swags, and festoons, as in the two illustrated.

To some extent the dish-ring was to the Irish what the dish-cross was to the English table. As a means for keeping food hot, the dish cross (see illustration on opposite page) is particularly convenient, as the bars are fitted to revolve, and the sliding sockets can be adjusted to any size dish.

Decanter stands, or coasters, three of which are shown, were an important item in the silver of the Georgian and early Victorian days. They were brought to the table after the ladies had left and the cloth was removed; and many bucks of the day were expert in coasting the decanter stand along the table; which accounts for their having a wooden bottom covered with baize and for the name, coaster. One or more of them are occasionally mounted on small silver wheels, presumably for the benefit of those who were less efficient in the coasting. For some time, they were out of fashion, but during the last few years their value has been recognized and today they are in more general use.

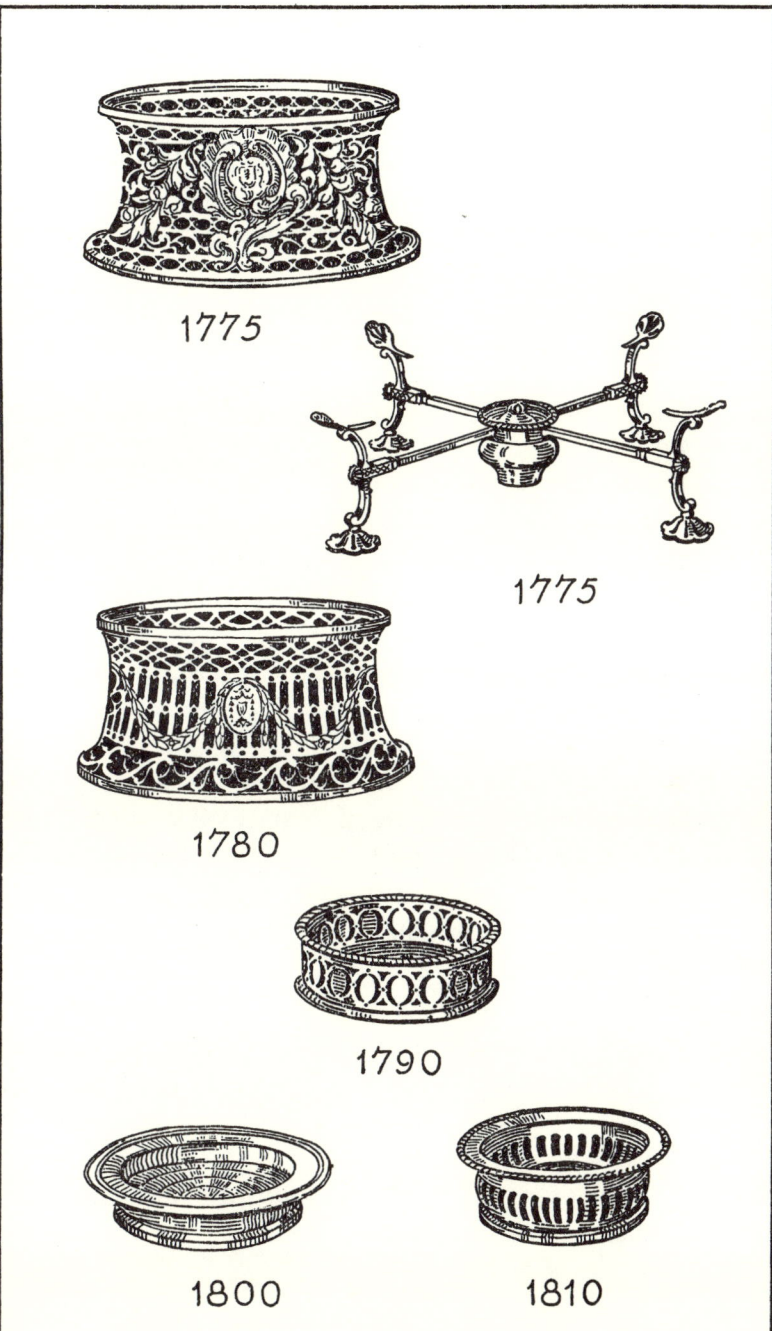

Two-Handled Cups

It is doubtful who really first suggested two-handled cups as trophies for horse racing and similar events, but Charles II was most probably responsible when, as the first English king to run horses in his own name, he substituted a silver cup, or bowl worth one hundred guineas, for the bell which up to that time had been the traditional prize.

This use of two-handled cups to commemorate some event or, more especially, as prizes for the winners of horse races became widely popular during the eighteenth century, some of the cups being made of gold. Those of the reigns of Queen Anne and George I are mostly quite plain, except for an engraved armorial insignia or inscription; and a large number of them were made without covers, as the one of 1705 shown on the opposite page. Many of them were the work of Irish silversmiths and are fitted with the harp-shaped handles, also seen in the illustration. This shaped handle does not necessarily indicate Irish silverwork, as it is found with English two-handled cups.

The cup and cover of 1720 is a type which was popular during the first part of the eighteenth century. The bowl follows closely that of the Queen Anne cup of 1705, but the handles are a simple scroll with a leaf form on the top of each, while the domical cover is not dissimilar to those of the contemporary coffee-pots. The example of 1770 demonstrates how, when a variation was made in some form or shape, it was applied to all similar objects, the narrowing in of the lower part of the bowl being the undulating line already mentioned in connexion with tea-pots and tea-kettles. The cup of 1795 also illustrates the application of a new style to similar objects; for this shape which is in the form of a classic vase appears with urns, hot-water jugs and other articles illustrated in the book.

Tankards, Mugs, and Goblets

London housewives in Elizabethan days drew their water from conduits that flowed along the principal streets; and the water was carried in large iron-bound wooden pitchers, known as tankards, from which the massive silver drinking vessels took their name. The tall tapering horn-shape of the first English tankards is especially similar to the water carriers, the iron hoops being repeated by ornamental bands.

During the Early Stuart period, the tankards became shorter and wider, and they gradually increased in size, until those of the Restoration period and William and Mary are upward of 8 inches high and 6 inches in diameter. The more popular late seventeenth-century tankards have a plain body with a small molding round the base, (this retains something of the ancient horn shape in the slight taper) a cover with flat top above, a convex member, and a scroll handle; an example of 1690 is illustrated on the opposite page.

This flat-top variety remained popular during the early years of Queen Anne's reign, but in about 1710, the flat top was superseded by the dome shape cover, though the body remains plain and the handle is unchanged. This style was fashionable until the reign of George III, though some few variations occur; the cover is sometimes slightly higher with more molded members than the one of 1725 shown, and a molded band is added round the body.

In the later eighteenth century, the straight-sided tankard was replaced by the taller bulbous shape reminiscent of the pear-shaped coffee-pots. This type retains nothing of the earlier straight-sided tankards. The cover is a high molded dome, the handle is a more ambitious recurving scroll in place of the simple

1690

1695

1725

1775

TANKARDS, MUGS AND GOBLETS

tapering scroll, and the flat bottom is replaced by a molded spreading foot, again similar to that of the pear-shaped coffee-pots.

As mugs for beer-drinking are, at different periods, smaller copies of the tankards, but without covers, this might suggest their having been intended for those with only a limited ability to consume beer. They are rarely more than about 5 inches high, and some of them only 3 inches.

The mug of 1695 illustrated, would perhaps seem to contradict the suggestion that mugs were copies of tankards. It does not, however, for the first tankards have a bellied body with a short neck quite similar in outline to this mug. The likeness of the tapering straight-sided mug of 1710, to the tankards of 1725 is obvious, though the mug has molded bands round the body; and the same applies to the bulbous shaped mug on a foot and the tankard of 1775.

The two goblets on the opposite page may be said to represent an eighteenth-century revival of the wine cup of the 1675 period. Until Elizabethan times, wine was served in the great cups from which both the host and the guests drank, a custom which was discontinued when the small individual wine cups, or goblets became fashionable. In time, the glass wine "goblets" replaced the silver ones, but a variety of the latter were made during the last part of the eighteenth century. Most of these have the rather large conical shaped bowl on a stem with round or square molded foot, and it is probable that goblets of this type were intended for beer rather than for wine. And the fact that some of them have a gadroon mount round the rim, which would not be particularly comfortable when drinking, would suggest that occasionally the Late Georgian goblets were trophies for minor races and other sports.

Punch-Bowls and Monteiths

These great bowls are one of the several magnificent silver objects associated with the ceremony of drinking; and, from the Late Stuart times until the early nineteenth century, at least one large punch bowl was part of the household silver in every wealthy family. In these less revelrous days, we are apt to see them more often filled with flowers in the centre of a large dining table, and used in this way their beauty is undeniable.

They are usually about twelve inches in diameter and proportionately deep, and a large number of them are quite plain, except for, perhaps, an engraved band round the rim, or a coat of arms. During the later Georgian period, they tend to become somewhat larger, while the body and foot are sometimes engraved and the rim ornamented with a gadroon and shell, or other mount.

Where they have the scalloped rim, as in the example of 1700 on the opposite page, the bowls are more elaborate. The body will be fluted, or otherwise decorated with chased and engraved work, the edges of the shaped rim mounted with scrolls, foliage and cherub heads, and, as a rule, a heavy handle held in a cast lion head is fitted to each side of the bowl. Bowls having this shaped rim, which is often removable, are referred to as monteiths — supposedly after a Scotchman named Monteigh who wore a cloak with a scalloped border.

Some Late Stuart punch-bowls have deeply notched rims, the purpose of which was to allow the wine glasses to hang by the stem inside the punch bowl; and this is the supposed purpose of the monteith rim. Whether the intention was to protect the glasses from breakage when they were carried into the room, or that the bowl was filled with water to warm, or cool the glasses, is debatable.

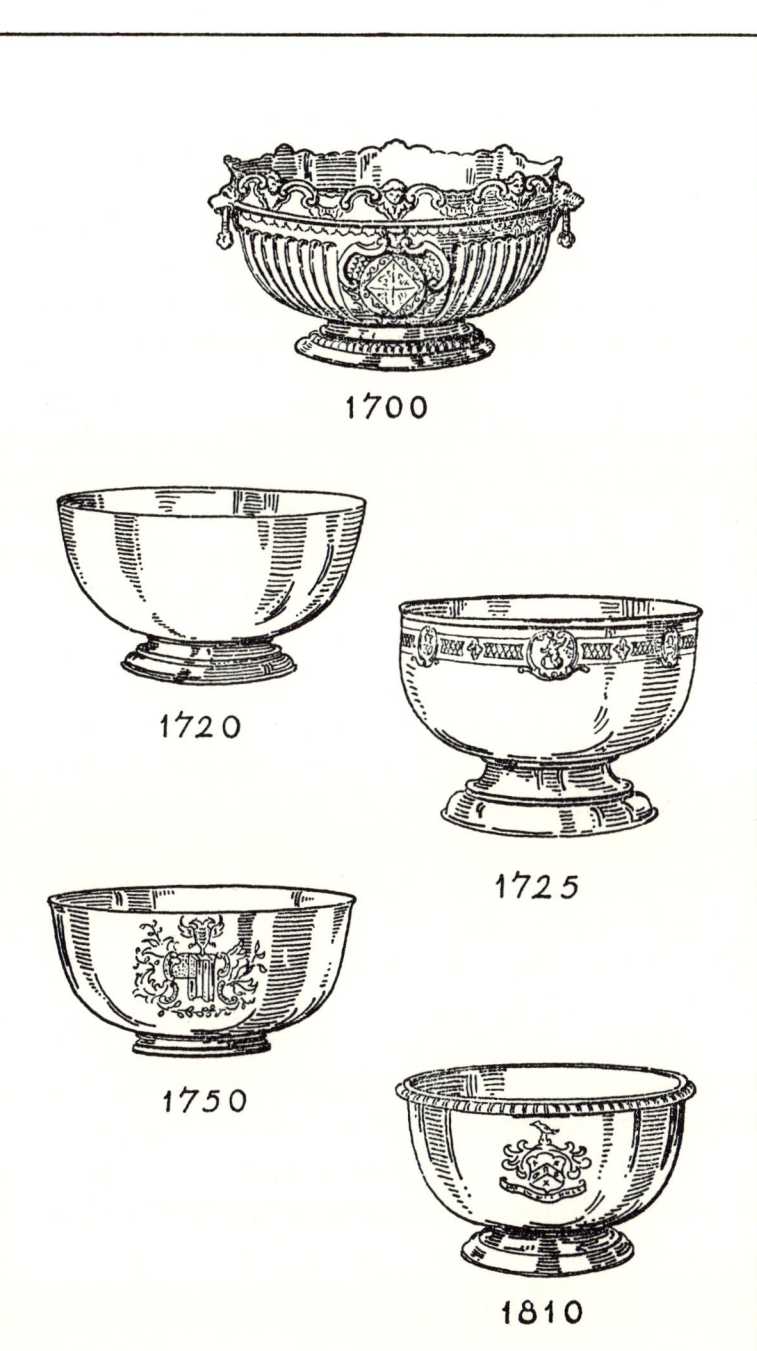

Candlesticks and Candelabra

True it is that having tried the novel we invariably travel back along the path of time to seek that which is innately beautiful. And one of the several discoveries we have made along that path is the charm of soft candlelights at the dinner-table. Whether a large or small table, a pair of silver candelabra, or a group of candlesticks adds an atmosphere of romance to the setting, and brings a sense of pleasant intimacy to the gathering.

None of the candlesticks made before the time of William and Mary would be suitable for a present-day house — even if they were obtainable; the few that survive are merely museum curiosities. But after 1680, when the merchant families began to furnish their house in a really comfortable manner, the candlesticks with fluted columns on square or octagonal bases were in fairly general use, an example of 1685 being shown on the opposite page.

Some ten years later when card-playing and gaming became generally fashionable, another type of candlestick with a smaller base made its appearance. This type is cast, and, consequently, a quite substantial piece of silver, the suggestion being that it found favor because the smaller base fitted the dished corners intended to hold candlesticks at the corners of the card tables. The stem, as can be seen in the one of 1695 illustrated, is formed of several members, the largest of which is noticeably cup-shape; and from then until the coming of the neo-classic styles, the candlesticks have numerous variations of the baluster stem and different molded bases.

Seven examples of the baluster stem are illustrated; in that of 1715 the shaft, while retaining the baluster form, is hexagonal, the socket is ornamented with triangular facets, and the base is also faceted. A similar hexagonal stem, but with a plainer, molded base is shown in the candlestick of 1750, while that of 1735 is another variation from the last mentioned; however, the

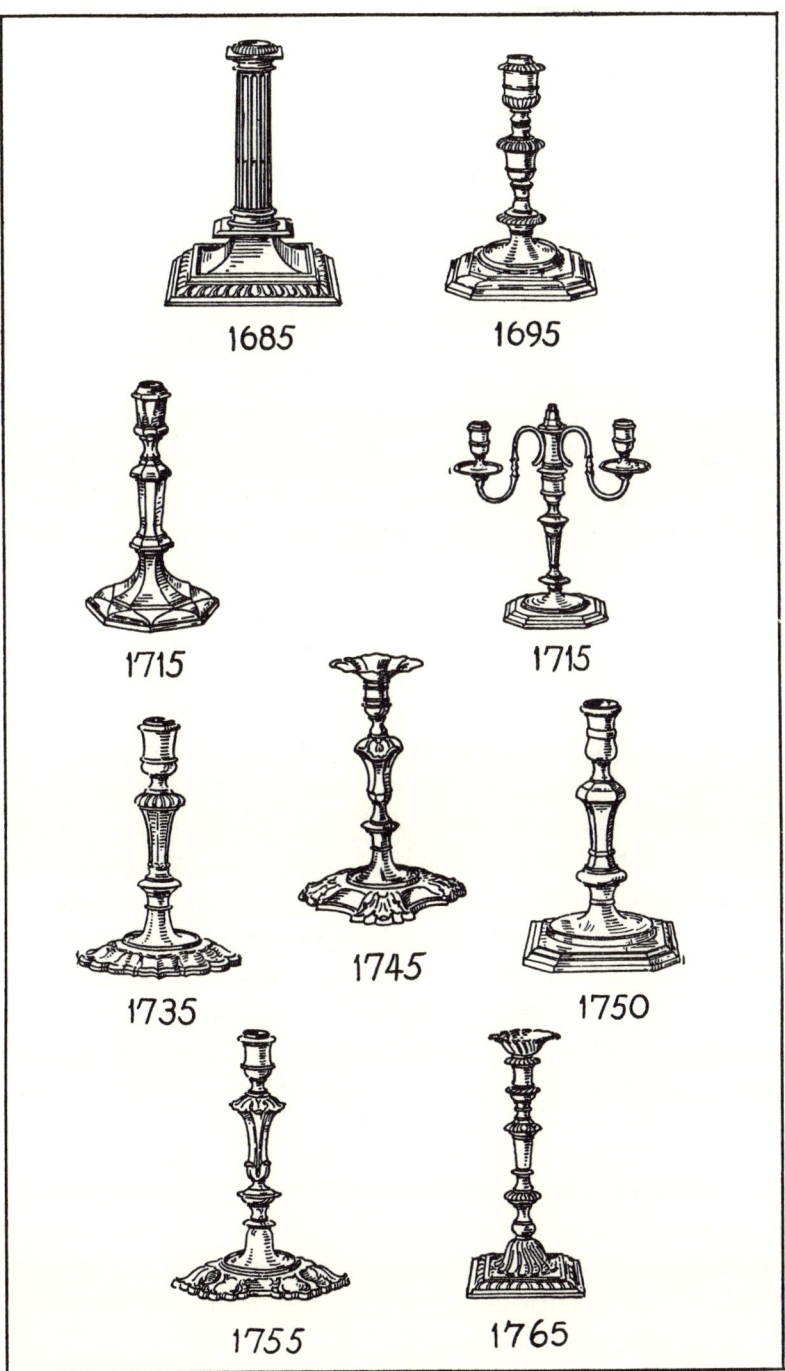

CANDLESTICKS AND CANDELABRA

facets are restricted to the upper part of the shaft with ornamental lobes on the shoulder and the base has a wavy outline.

Each of the other three (1745, 1755, and 1765) is slightly more ornamental, but each shows a variation of the baluster stem at a different period. The larger member in the stem of the first shows a resemblance to that of ten years earlier, but the top is ornamented at the four corners by acanthus leaves and the base which is shaped is similarly ornamented. A further development of the same outline is the 1755 example; but in that of 1765, the shaft is lighter with gadroon on each member, the high foot is ornamented with spiral lobes, and the base which is square also has a gadroon molding. Each of these several styles, therefore, represents a fairly well defined period during the first half of the eighteenth century.

After about 1765, there is an entire change in the styles of candlesticks, which like those of other silver, followed the neo-classic designs of Robert Adam the architect. Three examples of this period are illustrated at the top of the opposite page. That of 1770 has the columnar shaft and capital of the Corinthian style of architecture, a type of candlestick much favoured during the late eighteenth century. Another typically Adam candlestick has a square shaft, the sides of which are concave and taper toward the base; the base is square and ornamented with swags and similar classic forms are applied to the shaft and socket (see example of 1775). The shaft of the candlestick of 1790 is in the form of an inverted cone, and is one of the modified classic styles popular during the first quarter of the nineteenth century.

Having dealt with candlesticks, there is no need to touch at length upon candelabra; but it might be observed that as candelabra may be transformed into candlesticks by the removal of the branches when necessary, so any suitable candlestick will serve as the base for branches.

Bedroom-Candlesticks, Taper-Jacks, and Snuffers

To most present-day city dwellers, the old tray candlestick is merely a relic of a forgotten past; but there are houses along the countryside of England where they are still to be found on the hall table to light the sometimes stumbling feet to bed.

They differ little in style, for each has a short socket fitted in a wide tray with a handle and a small conical extinguisher. Some, such as the one of 1775 illustrated, have a slot in the stem to accommodate a pair of snuffers, which were necessary to cut off the charred wick of the old tallow candles. As a rule, however, the snuffers, accompanied by a small silver tray, were separate, and there was generally one of these in each room for snuffing the candles in the table candlesticks and the wall sconces. Admittedly the bedroom candlesticks are unnecessary in the modern house, but one or two on a dressing table are attractive and romantic ornaments; and one of the little silver snuffer trays, such as is shown at the bottom of the opposite page, might well accompany the candlesticks as a pin tray.

The other object, perhaps to many curious, is a taper-jack and was one of the several essentials on a writing table before the days of gummed envelopes, when letters were sealed with wax. The coil of taper was placed on a spindle and the end passed through the small socket at the top, which was lighted when required for melting sealing wax. There are also a variety of small cylindrical boxes with a chimney-like top through which the end of the taper coil was passed, the coil itself being in the box; another style was globe shape formed of silver wire on a spreading foot. Most of these taper-jacks and boxes date from the end of the eighteenth century; an example of either type, however, is not often met with, and when one is offered, it is well worth acquiring.

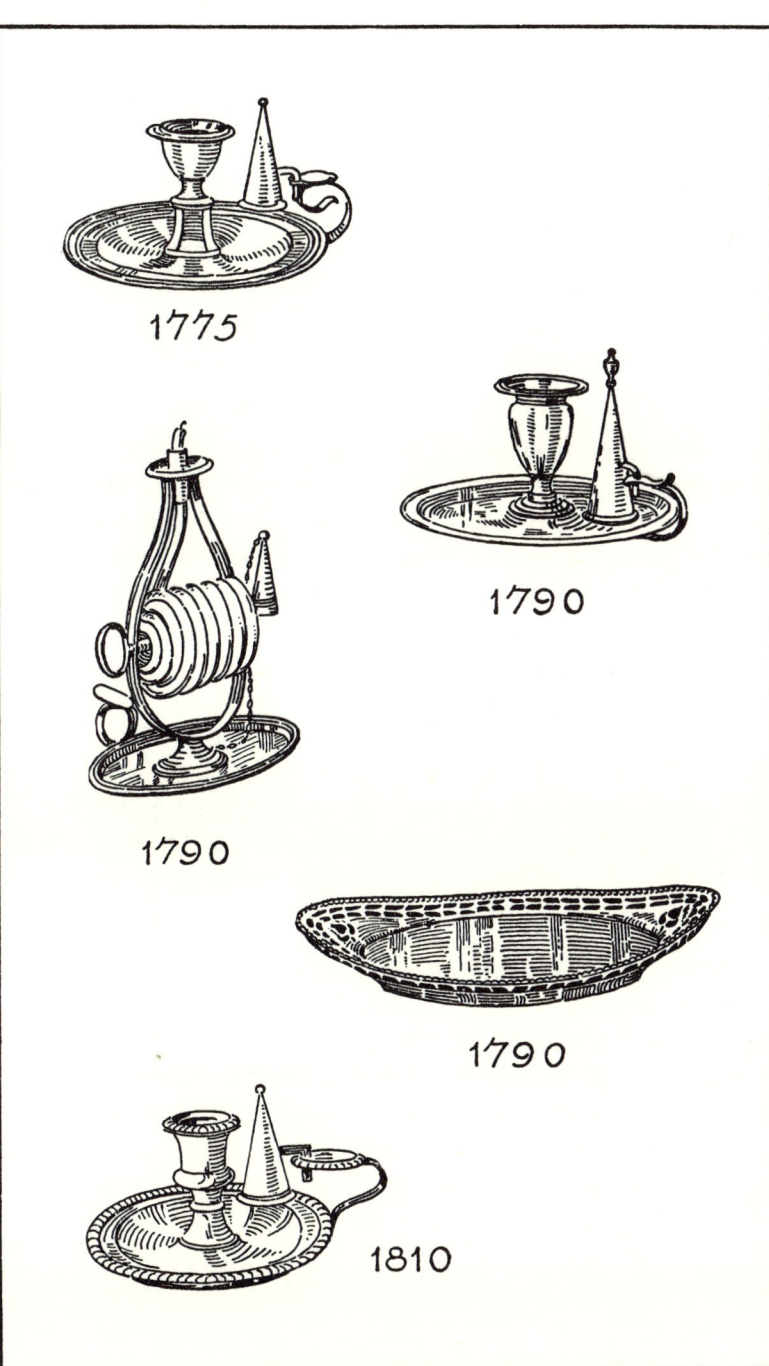

Inkstands

Probably no single article of household silver indicates in its evolution more social changes than the inkstand, or standish, which was its original name. All these changes took place in the nineteenth century, when the accidental discovery of blotting paper about 1820 displaced the caster which held sand to dry the ink; the introduction of envelopes with adhesive flaps (about 1840) dispensed with the necessity for wafer-boxes and taper-holders; and the invention of steel pens (about 1850) made the pen-pot superfluous.

Every inkstand of earlier than the first part of the last century is equipped with three or more of the following articles; an ink-pot, a sand-box, a pen-pot, a wafer-box, a taper-holder, a bell; yet each of these, except the inkpot, is unnecessary to the modern writing table. Compare the four inkstands illustrated; each has a large tray, or dish, one has a raised edge and each of the others a groove for the stick of sealing-wax. The one of 1750 is fitted with only an inkpot, a pen-pot and a small taper-holder, the original user of this therefore had a separate sand-caster for "blotting" his letters. Many casters formerly used for sand, today serve as sugar-casters. That of 1765 has an inkpot with holes for quill-pens, a sand-caster and a wafer box under the taper-holder; and the one of 1790 two pots and a sand-caster, while the fourth is fitted similarly to that of 1765.

When a bell is part of the accessories, it is placed in the centre, its purpose being to summon a servant; this bell, however, occurs only with the earlier inkstands, and was later replaced by the taper-holder, which until then had been separate. Most of the taper-holders are miniature copies of the various styles of baluster stem candlesticks; others, known as taper-boxes and taper-jacks, are referred to on another page.

After about 1760, cut-glass pots with silver mounts in silver sockets were used in place of the former silver ones, as shown in the three later examples illustrated.

1750

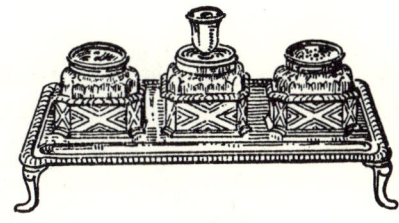

1765

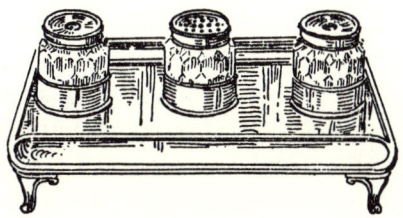

1790

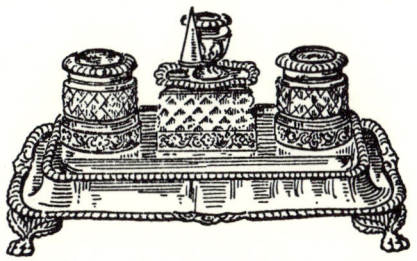

1815

Spoons, Forks, and Knives

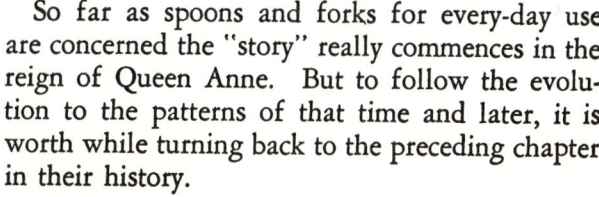

So far as spoons and forks for every-day use are concerned the "story" really commences in the reign of Queen Anne. But to follow the evolution to the patterns of that time and later, it is worth while turning back to the preceding chapter in their history.

The first type of spoon with a flat stem was introduced during the second half of the seventeenth century, when the top was notched in two places in the form known as the trifid; it was at this time, too, that the tongue, or rat-tail, was added to the back of the bowl—the intention of this being to strengthen the handle.

Toward the end of the century, the notches were discontinued, and the end was shaped rather like an arch similar to the mirror and door panels of the William and Mary period. The end of the stem is turned toward the inside of the bowl, and the bowl itself tends to become narrower.

Early in the reign of Queen Anne, the spoons developed to a shape which is more generally familiar at the present time. The top of the "arch" outline disappeared and was replaced by the plain rounded end, and the former flat stem was made slightly thicker with a ridge well down the inside of the stem. The rat-tail on back of the bowl remained and the top was still turned toward the inside of the bowl. This is the first evolution towards what is known as the Old English pattern.

This style was popular until the end of George II's reign, when the rat-tail was omitted and replaced by a rounded drop which appears on the Old English and other later patterns. The ridge on the underside of the stem was also changed, for while it did not disappear entirely, it became much shorter. About the middle of the eighteenth century, there was a vogue for ornamenting

SPOONS, FORKS, AND KNIVES

the backs of the bowls with rococo motifs such as shells and foliated scrolls, but examples of these are not often met with today.

Then came a new style of stem which is almost unknown now; yet it was one which had an important influence on the later spoon patterns. It has been called the Onslow pattern, after a prominent parliamentarian of the reign of George II. The bowl remains egg-shape as before, but the top of the stem ends in the form of a volute scroll; this scroll, instead of turning up toward the inside of the bowl, as the stem does in other earlier spoons, turns down toward the back. And this change was adopted in the stems of all later patterns.

Of these later patterns, that known as the Old English is unquestionably foremost. It appeared in about 1760 and became immediately popular, a popularity it has never lost. The stem of the Old English pattern spoons and forks has the rounded top similar in outline to that of the Queen Anne period. But unlike the Queen Anne, it has no ridge on the inside of the stem, though a trace of this remains at the end which now turns down toward the back of the bowl; and there is another sign of the early eighteenth-century spoon in the slight thickening of the end. This, it is suggested, may have originated from hammering over the pointed section of the William III shaped top stem, and so forming the first round end stem.

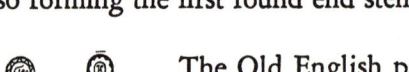

The Old English pattern, while more often plain, was frequently ornamented. Two of the simpler forms of ornamentation is a beaded edge and the thread edge round the stem but these styles lack the beauty of the finely engraved stems which are keenly sought today, though it cannot be said that a complete service is easy to find.

Probably the two most popular engraved styles are known as the bright-cut and the feather edge. Bright-

SPOONS, FORKS, AND KNIVES

cut is a series of deeply cut zig-zag lines, a form of ornamentation that has survived from quite primitive ages. It is engraved round the edges of the stems of spoons and forks in a continuous line of slightly extended zig-zags, and within this border there is another line of lightly engraved and closer zig-zags—the nearest simile that comes to mind is a zipper fastener. Feather-edge is also a narrow band at the edge of and following the shape of the stem, the center of this pattern being left plain; it gets its name from the fact that the engraved oblique lines form a feather-like design, and it is an instance where a very effective design is achieved by a quite simple method.

Ornamentation was applied also to the backs of the bowls, especially to the tea-spoons which were made in sets for gifts. These desirable sets exhibit a wide variety of motifs ranging from ships in full sail to flowers, oak leaves and others. On some of the bowls there are cryptic designs occasionally accompanied by mottoes, and these suggest that spoons were made and decorated to commemorate a particular episode or event.

Little need be said of the fiddle pattern, and its several offsprings such as the shell and thread; but it is interesting to recall that the first sign of the fiddle pattern occurs with the Old English.

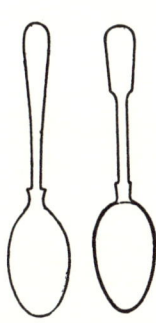

This was in about 1775 when some of the Old English pattern spoons — even those with engraved stems — assumed the small angular shoulders near the bowl; these being one of the features with the fiddle pattern of the nineteenth century.

The old English pattern spoons with the shoulders while not plentiful are met with, and those with the plain stem are attractive. The bowls are similar in size and shape to the usual

[81]

SPOONS, FORKS, AND KNIVES

Old English, but the stems are noticeably narrower, and the drop where the stem joins the bowl is flatter. It would seem likely that more of these spoons were made by provincial silversmiths, because it is not uncommon to find them without marks.

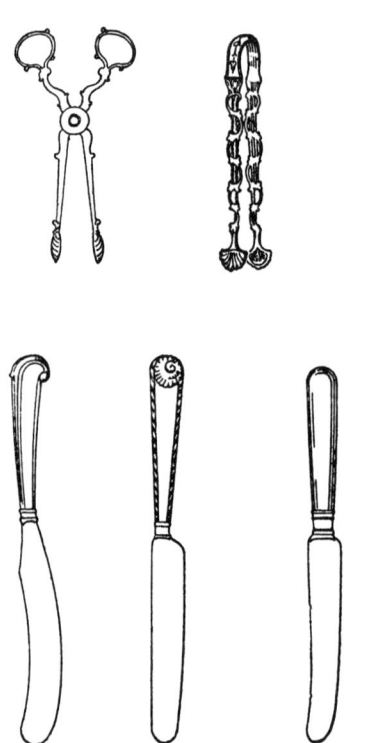

The scissor tong of the first quarter of the 18th century was followed by the elaborate open-work Chippendale spring tong. The lighter weight simpler type is to be had plain or engraved.

The knife shown here has the pistol handle of plain design. This style continued in popularity from the first quarter of the 18th century into George III period when it becomes ornate with scrolls and leaf decoration. The straight handle followed this and is to be found in the design of the forks and spoons with which it was used.

With forks, we may perhaps indulge in a few brief historical observations, for compared with spoons they are a "novelty." Actually, table forks were, to all intents, unknown in England until the latter part of the seventeenth century, though they had been in use for eating at table in several of the Continental countries for many years previous.

SPOONS, FORKS, AND KNIVES

The first has three prongs, but some with four prongs were also made during the time of Charles II; at this time, they had the flat stem with a trifid top. There are also small forks made in the time of Queen Anne and slightly earlier which have only two prongs, but these are rarities indeed. All the forks of the first part of the eighteenth century are small, but after that time they are noticeably larger, and later in the century, the two sizes which we know as table-forks and dessert-forks were in everyday use; the stems throughout being similar to those of the contemporary spoons.

There is one "relative" of forks which though in general use until the nineteenth century has disappeared from the table, and that is the skewer used to hold joints of meat in shape; and the larger ones are more convenient in carving than a carving fork. Admittedly, skewers do not rank as artistic silverwork yet they meet with quite a keen demand, especially those with the beveled edges which are today frequently used as paper knives.

And there is a "cousin" of the spoon which is worthy of mention, namely the marrow scoop. The more common pattern of these little understood articles is about 9 inches long with a wide elongated spoon bowl at one end, and a long narrow stem which is deeply fluted. These were used for extracting the marrow from bones in the days when marrow on toast was a more fashionable dish than it is today; but if it is no longer fashionable, it is still a delicacy, and there is a certain pleasurable amusement in using such a "novelty" as a marrow scoop at a modern table. But they are now more often used as honey spoons, for which they are specially suitable.

The Assay Office in 1683

1. The Assayer
2. The Scales
3. The Cases for Weights

Changes Within One Century

Exactly one hundred years elapsed between the time the small bowl below and the large dish on the next page were made, and seven monarchs had reigned in England. And it is interesting to follow the improvement in both style and workmanship during that hundred years.

Silver bowls, such as that of 1675, were used for tasting wine, but were replaced during the eighteenth century by glasses. They are about 3 inches in diameter at the rim and quite shallow; and being of thin silver they were decorated with various rather crudely punched flowers, leaves and other forms to stiffen the metal.

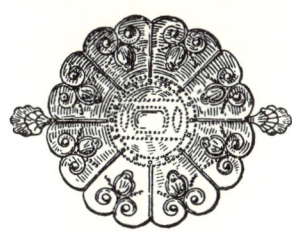

When we speak of saucers in our time, we generally refer to those used with tea-cups. Actually these derived their name from dishes (similar to the one of 1685) which, in the seventeenth century were used to hold sauces, sweetmeats or fruit. Like the tasters, they are of thin silver, and for the same reason, are embossed with ribs to form panels which in turn are embossed with scrolls and a clumsy outline of some fruit, the center being punched with a circle of beads enclosing other forms and a shield. But the very primitive nature of the decoration adds to the charm of these now quite rare dishes of the Stuart times.

In actual time, it is but a short space from this Stuart saucer to the Georgian fruit dish of 1730; but the difference in the style and workmanship is very noticeable. These circular dishes, which are often called strawberry-dishes, are larger than those of the seventeenth century, and though manifesting a more advanced technique, retain traces of the earlier dish in the scalloped and ribbed edge. They are slightly deeper than a plate and though generally plain are occasionally engraved. The Dublin silversmiths produced a number of plain ones, and these, too, have the scalloped and ribbed border.

[85]

CHANGES WITHIN ONE CENTURY

Another smaller dish which was used to hold butter balls or sweet meats was the scallop shell, of which one is shown. 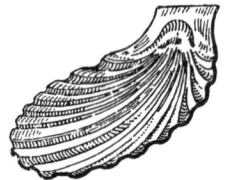 These were introduced during the Early Georgian period and were popular until the beginning of the following century. They are by no means plentiful, though single examples, and, sometimes pairs are obtainable.

Our modern word "dish" has an unromantic sound. The  ancient "charger" for the large silver dishes, such as the one shown, would be far more poetic; and in truth they are the modern counterpart of the charger, on which the joint was carried to the table in medieval times, in the same way that meat plates were the wooden trenchers of long ago. Dishes of this type were made in various sizes up to 25 inches; those for the joint generally having shallow groves which allow the gravy to flow into a small well, often referred to as "well and tree" dishes. These were part of the large Georgian silver dinner services which frequently comprised as many as 200 pieces. In style, they vary little; the dishes and plates are occasionally shaped and the mounts sometimes more elaborate than the gadroon, but the gadroon was then, as now, the most favored style.

Examples of a vinaigrette, a nut-meg box and a snuff box shown here, are representative of types.

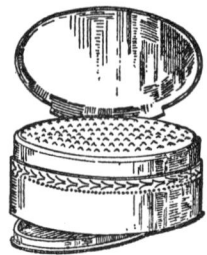 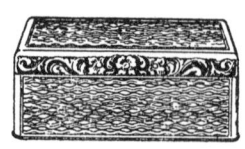 

Reminders of Past Traditions

Illustrations are shown of various articles of household silver, many of which represent long-forgotten customs; but if these customs have fallen into disuse, many of the silver objects associated with them serve for other purposes even in these less romantic and less picturesque days.

This beautiful box of 1700, for example, at one time adorned 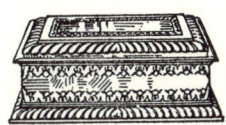 the dressing table of some aristocratic English lady, when it was doubtless part of a magnificent toilet service. Many of these toilet services have been dispersed, but all the different pieces find a use in a modern house; boxes similar to that illustrated being equally useful today, for small jewelry as they were more than two centuries ago. And  a small shallow circular box of the type, also shown on the opposite page, will by having a mirror fitted to the inside of the lid, make a unique compact.

There are certain pieces of early silver which are essentially  Irish both in origin and character, and the small pierced dish with a pierced cover is one. These attractive and now rare dishes are oval, about 7 inches long, and they invariably have a knob in the form of a cow on the cover. The sides of some of them are pierced and chased with rustic scenes, in which a milkmaid milking a cow, a windmill, and similar objects figure. In these days, butter is rarely placed on the table in one large piece, but these charming little dishes, which of course have a glass liner, are frequently used to hold chocolates, or preserves.

The small silver beehive is one of the several conceits which the eighteenth and early nineteenth century silversmiths produced.

REMINDERS OF PAST TRADITIONS

It is really a honey pot and many of those now available bear the mark of Paul Storr.

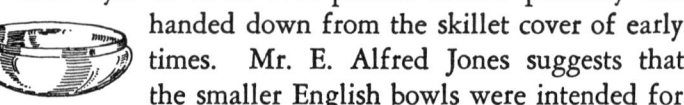

In the United States, the shallow vessel with a single flat pierced handle is known as a porringer, but those with a smaller bowl, which were made in England, are commonly called "bleeding-bowls". This style of bowl with pierced handle probably was handed down from the skillet cover of early times. Mr. E. Alfred Jones suggests that the smaller English bowls were intended for wine-tasters, and there is much to support this contention. The

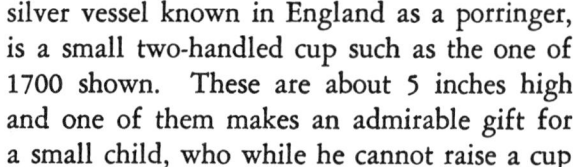

silver vessel known in England as a porringer, is a small two-handled cup such as the one of 1700 shown. These are about 5 inches high and one of them makes an admirable gift for a small child, who while he cannot raise a cup which has only one handle can do so when there is one for each of his chubby hands.

Like the oblong box referred to previously, the delicate little two-handled bowl and stand of 1700 are probably relics of an important toilet service. The bowl is engraved with scrolls, and the lower part ornamented with cut-card work, that is, shapes, such as leaves, cut from thin sheet silver, (as one would cut them with scissors from cardboard) and applied to the bowl. A complete original eighteenth century silver toilet service comprised at least twenty pieces, including two low bowls and two tazza-shaped stands such as those illustrated, two small jars and covers, two large oblong boxes, four small boxes, two bottles, candlesticks, snuffers and tray, and various other articles.

Those who are fortunate owners of an early porcelain tea-service which includes some of the small bowls which were the forerunners of the tea-cup with a handle, will recognize the small

REMINDERS OF PAST TRADITIONS

silver bowl and saucer of 1725. Silver tea-bowls of this form copied from the Chinese porcelain tea-bowls were made during  the first part of the eighteenth century; very few have been preserved, however, for when porcelain tea-ware began to be made in England, in about 1750, the silver tea-bowls went to the melting pot. While of great rarity "things" of this nature are of great interest to the collector.

In the notes on salvers and waiters, reference was made to 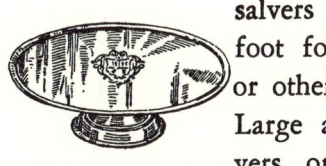 salvers on a stem and foot for "giving Beer or other liquid thing". Large and ornate salvers, or tazze as they are often termed, were made in the reign of Charles II as stands for the large two-handled cups. Later they became smaller and more simple in style with a plain center and a molded or gadroon edge, as those of 1685 and 1715 illustrated, and were used in serving a glass of wine. They would introduce a certain romance if used for that purpose at a present-day gathering, though they are more practical as stands for cake or sandwiches. And with a suitable two-handled cup one of the eighteenth century salvers is an unusual and effective center ornament on a dining table.

The George II small bowl is a wine cup known as a tumbler, because having a rounded bottom, it rocks and tumbles. Bowls  of this type will not fall over, however, because, in making them, the craftsmen hammered the silver so that the bottom is thicker and heavier than the sides. They were made in various sizes, but none of them is very large. If perhaps

REMINDERS OF PAST TRADITIONS

slightly alarming to anyone drinking from one for the first time, the smaller ones are coming into fashion again in England for sherry.

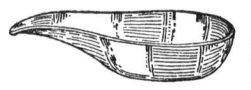 The curious, rather helpless looking little bowl with a spout, is known as a pap-boat and was used to feed infants and quite possibly invalids. It can be adapted to one of many modern uses today.

 Associated with the convivial ceremony of punch-making there are several small articles such as the long handled ladles for filling the jugs from the bowl, and the lemon-strainers. The ladles were made in large numbers as they were needed equally for the large porcelain bowls brought from China, but strainers are relatively rare. Some of the latter are quite elaborate, and in place of the plain wire handles, have two finely pierced and shaped handles similar to those of American porringers.

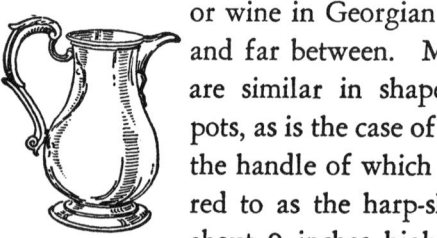 Silver jugs of a size that may have been used to hold punch or wine in Georgian times exist, but they are few and far between. Most of those that are known are similar in shape to the pear-shaped coffee-pots, as is the case of the 1770 example illustrated, the handle of which is the shape frequently referred to as the harp-shape. These jugs which are about 9 inches high are generally catalogued as beer-jugs, for which they are admirably suited, but in these days of bottled ale, they are more generally used as water pitchers.

REMINDERS OF PAST TRADITIONS

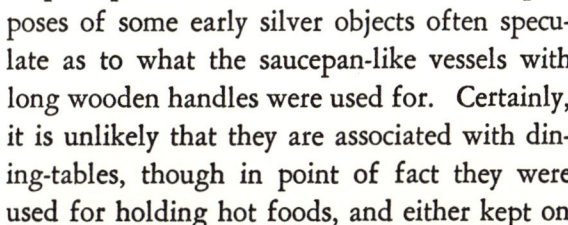

Those who are perhaps not familiar with the former purposes of some early silver objects often speculate as to what the saucepan-like vessels with long wooden handles were used for. Certainly, it is unlikely that they are associated with dining-tables, though in point of fact they were used for holding hot foods, and either kept on the stove in the kitchen until served, or placed on the sideboard over a spirit lamp. This method of serving food was fashionable well into the last century, for until fairly modern times, the kitchens of the great English houses were often some distance from the dining-room. These same saucepans are still used occasionally to heat a small quantity of food or liquid, and, to some extent, represent what to past generations was the chafing dish of modern times.

One other reminder of the customs of our forefathers stands on many a present-day sideboard in the form of a pair of wine-coolers; perhaps they are only occasionally used now for the original purpose, but they are beautiful and dignified ornaments none the less. Before these small wine-coolers were introduced from France in the time of William III, wine at a social gathering was cooled in huge silver cisterns, which contained the ice in which the bottles were put to cool. The later wine-cooler, is rather like a large vase on a foot, such as is illustrated. This type is fitted with a movable rim and jacket that fits the bottle, the space between the jacket and the wall of the vase being packed with ice. By far the larger number of this style date from the late eighteenth and early nineteenth centuries, and some of them are quite massive objects with elaborate applied decorations.

Royal Arms

WILLIAM AND MARY

QUEEN ANNE

GEORGE I

GEORGE III

Notes on Silver Marks

Many subjects when set out in tabulated form are often regarded by the layman as highly technical, but when the salient features are analysed and separately explained, what was obscure is clarified. And the following notes, it is hoped, will help to clarify the meaning of the seemingly meaningless heiroglyphics of the marks reproduced in following pages.

Marks on London Silver.

Since silver was first marked in London, in 1400, seven different marks have been used at different periods; and with the exception of the sovereign's head, each of these marks—with certain minor variations—is in use at the present time. In the order of their first being adopted these are:—

The leopard's head crowned.
Date Letter.
Maker's mark.
Lion passant.
Figure of Britannia.
Lion's Head erased.
Reigning sovereign's head.

The variations occur with the leopard head, which in 1821 loses its crown and has remained uncrowned since; and in the same year the walking lion instead of being full face is shown in profile. The sovereign's head first appeared in 1784 to indicate the payment of duty, but on the duty being abolished in 1890, this mark is discontinued.

Both the figure of Britannia and the lion's head erased were adopted in 1697, from which year until 1719-20 they replaced the crowned leopard's head and the lion passant. These indicate a standard of silver higher than that known as Sterling—in other words it contained a smaller portion of alloy. The reason why the English Government changed the standard for household silver was this: In Charles the Second's reign there had been such a shortage of metal that the silversmiths melted down the

NOTES ON SILVER MARKS

coinage which was of Sterling standard. To prevent this, a higher standard of silver was ordered for all silverwork—the coinage being left as before. And the old marks used by the Assay Office were discontinued and replaced by the Britannia and the lion's head erased. In 1719, the old Sterling standard was restored and the leopard's head and lion passant marks reappeared; but the Britannia and lion's head remained legal for silver of the higher standard, and are in force to the present time.

One of the hall-marks on every piece of silver that has been assayed in London, is a single letter—known as the date letter; it is by this that the actual year is determined. There is one particular type of letter for each cycle of twenty years, during which the whole alphabet in proper sequence (excepting J, V, W, X, Y, Z, which are omitted by the London Assay Office) is used to denote consecutive years in that cycle. The style of the letters is changed at the beginning of every cycle; and to prevent confusion that might arise from the obvious necessity to repeat the types of letters at intervals, the shape of the shield in which the letters appear is varied. Consequently, in studying the letters, it is advisable to pay closer attention to the outline of the punch than might at first seem necessary.

Another punch shows two (occasionally more) letters which indicate the name of the man who made the article. And here, too, there are some variations which are helpful in discovering the date of a silver object. Until 1697, the maker's mark is a symbol, or the initials of his given name and his surname. From 1697 to 1719-20, this was changed to the first two letters of his surname, thus: GA (Garthorne), LA (Lambe), Br (Brydon). In 1720, the initials were reinstituted; in 1740 the silversmiths were ordered to destroy their existing name punches and to use new ones, which were to be their initials in a type of letter different from any they had used previously.

It has been argued by some who have given but a cursory study to silver marks, that the use of the same letter to denote different years in the various cycles is confusing; which proves they have not studied the minor details. To better illustrate this, we will select small Roman letter b which denotes the years 1737, 1777, 1817 and 1897.

Now for the variations: firstly the shape of the date letter punches. There is, admittedly, some resemblance between those of 1777 and 1817, but that of 1737 is entirely different, and an example of a set of marks for each of the two years 1777 and 1817 will show that despite the similarity between two of the punches, there is no possible chance of confusion.

For 1777 the marks would be: the crowned leopard's head—the lion full face—the date letter b (in a straight top shield)—the maker's initials.

And for 1817: the crowned leopard's head—the lion full face—the date letter b (in a shield with the top corners clipped)—the maker's initials—and the important additional identification of the king's head.

So assuming that all the other marks were more closely similar than they are, there is the king's head to remove any doubt. Again assuming that the date letter b on an 1897 piece of silver to be in exactly the same shaped punch as the other years (which it is not) it is impossible to mistake it, because the leopard's head has no crown, the lion is in profile, and the sovereign's head is missing.

ENGLISH PROVINCIAL TOWN MARKS

Formerly, a considerable number of English towns used their own marks on silver made in the district, but only three remain active, namely Chester, Birmingham and Sheffield. In this brief summary we need not consider more than these three and three others namely, Exeter, Newcastle, and York; each of the last three assay offices was closed during the nineteenth century.

NOTES ON SILVER MARKS

The principal punch among those impressed on silver made in and around each of these provincial towns is the Town mark which is: for Chester, the word STERLING until 1700, three lions and three wheat-sheaves united until 1778, and since then three wheat-sheaves and a dagger. For Birmingham, an anchor; Sheffield, a crown; Exeter, a castle with three turreted towers; Newcastle, three castles placed two above one; and York, five lions passant on a Greek cross.

Other marks which accompany the Town marks are a date letter, the lion, the leopard's head (excepting Birmingham and Sheffield) and the maker's mark. There are other variations such as the figure of Britannia and the lion's head erased which appear with some of them, but these may be seen from the tabulated lists.

SCOTTISH MARKS

Besides Edinburgh and Glasgow which are still active, there are a number of marks used by other smaller towns in Scotland. Here, however, we may confine our interest to the two larger cities. The town mark of Edinburgh has always been—during the period we are concerned with—a three towered castle, and after 1746, the thistle is added in a separate punch. There is always a date letter, and until the thistle was added, the punches included the deacon's initials as well as those of the maker.

Similarly, the Glasgow town mark has always been a tree, a bird, a fish and a bell (combined in one punch), supposedly derived from the legend of the Queen of Caidyow's ring. After 1819, a lion rampant in a separate punch was added; also after that year a regular series of date letters was adopted. Other marks and minor variations will be discovered in the lists shown.

IRISH MARKS

Apart from the marks used by the Dublin Assay Office and the STERLING punch of Cork, there are no Irish marks that need be referred to here.

NOTES ON SILVER MARKS

The familiar harp punch has always been used to indicate silver marked at Dublin ever since the Goldsmith's Company of that city was granted a Charter in 1637; and during the period which this book covers (1675 — 1825), the harp is always crowned. Until 1730, only three marks are found on Dublin silver, namely, the harp crowned, the date letter, and the maker's initials; in that year, the figure of Hibernia was adopted to indicate the payment of duty. The only other punch found on Dublin silver is the reigning sovereign's head from 1807 to 1890.

There, Dublin silver bears three punches until 1730; four from 1731 until 1806; and five from 1807 until 1890.

Cork was formerly an important center for silverwork, owing to silver being mined in that part of Ireland during the early seventeenth century. Before about 1710, this town used a variety of marks on silver made there; but after that time the word STERLING in different forms was adopted. This word is almost invariably in capital letters, though of different sizes; also the spelling and the manner in which it is sometimes divided show several variations, STER(LING), STE(RLING), STARLING, STERLG, STERG, STIRLING, STER, all being used at different times. Occasionally, too, the word is incised, that is, punched into the silver in the same way as this same word is used to mark silver made in the United Stated at the present time.

Assay Marks

CHARLES II	1660-1684
JAMES II	1685-1687
WILLIAM & MARY	1688-1694
WILLIAM III	1695-1702
ANNE	1702-1713
GEORGE I	1714-1726
GEORGE II	1727-1759
GEORGE III	1760-1819
GEORGE IV	1820-1829

LONDON 1658-1836

	LEOPARD'S HEAD CROWNED.	DATE LETTER.	LION PASSANT.
1658-9	🦁	𝔄	🦁
1659-60	,,	𝔅	,,
CHAS. II. 1660-1	,,	ℭ	,,
1661-2	,,	𝔇	,,
1662-3	,,	𝔈	🦁
1663-4	,,	𝔉	,,
1664-5	,,	𝔊	,,
1665-6	,,	ℌ	,,
1666-7	,,	𝔍	,,
1667-8	,,	𝔎	,,
1668-9	🦁	𝔏	🦁
1669-70	,,	𝔐	,,
1670-1	,,	𝔑	,,
1671-2	,,	𝔒	,,
1672-3	,,	𝔓	,,
1673-4	,,	𝔔	,,
1674-5	,,	ℜ	,,
1675-6	,,	𝔖	,,
1676-7	,,	𝔗	,,
1677-8	,,	𝔘	,,

	LEOPARD'S HEAD CROWNED.	DATE LETTER.	LION PASSANT.
1678-9	🦁	𝔞	🦁
1679-80	,,	𝔟	🦁
1680-1	🦁	𝔠	🦁
1681-2	,,	𝔡	,,
1682-3	,,	𝔢	,,
1683-4	,,	𝔣	,,
1684-5	,,	𝔤	,,
JAS. II. 1685-6	,,	𝔥	,,
1686-7	,,	𝔦	,,
1687-8	,,	𝔨	,,
1688-9	,,	𝔩	,,
WM. & MY. 1689-90	🦁	𝔪	🦁
1690-1	,,	𝔫	,,
1691-2	,,	𝔬	,,
1692-3	,,	𝔭	,,
1693-4	,,	𝔮	,,
1694-5	,,	𝔯	,,
WM. III. 1695-6	,,	𝔰	,,
MAY 29, 1696, TO MCH. 27, 1697.	,,	𝔱	,,

Variations of date-letters of this cycle:

1664-5   1667-8

1671-2   1677-8

Date	BRIT. ANNIA.	DATE LETTER.	LION'S HEAD ERASED.
1697 MCH. 27 TO MAY 29.	🛡	🛡	🛡
1697-8	,,	B	,,
1698-9	,,	C	,,
1699/1700	🛡	D	🛡
1700-1	,,	E	,,
1701-2	,,	ff	,,
ANNE. 1702-3	,,	G	,,
1703-4	,,	H	,,
1704-5	,,	I	,,
1705-6	,,	K	,,
1706-7	,,	L	,,
1707-8	,,	M	,,
1708-9	,,	N	,,
1709-10	,,	O	,,
1710-11	,,	P	,,
1711-2	,,	Q	,,
1712-3	,,	R	,,
1713-4	,,	S	,,
GEO. I. 1714-5	,,	T	,,
1715-6	,,	V	,,

Date	BRIT. ANNIA.	DATE LETTER.	LION'S HEAD ERASED.
1716-7	🛡	A	🛡
1717-8	,,	B	,,
1718-9	,,	C	,,
	LEOPARD'S HEAD CROWNED		LION PASSANT.
1719-20	🛡	D	🛡
1720-1	,,	E	,,
1721-2	🛡	F	🛡
‡1722-3	,,	G	,,
1723-4	,,	H	,,
§1724-5	🛡	I	🛡
1725-6	,,	K	,,
1726-7	🛡	L L	🛡
GEO. II. ‖1727-8	,,	M M	,,
1728-9	,,	N	,,
1729-30	🛡	O	🛡
1730-1	,,	P	,,
1731-2	,,	Q	,,
1732-3	,,	R	,,
1733-4	,,	S	,,
1734-5	,,	T	,,
1735-6	,,	V	,,

	LEOPARD'S HEAD CROWNED	DATE LETTER	LION PASSANT			LEOPARD'S HEAD CROWNED	DATE LETTER	LION PASSANT
1736-7		a			1756-7		A	
1737-8	,,	b	,,		1757-8	,,	B	,,
1738-9	,,	c	,,		*1758-9	,,	C	,,
1739-40 {	,,	d	,,		*1759-60	,,	D	,,
		d			GEO. III. 1760-1	,,	E	,,
1740-1	,,	e	,,		1761-2	,,	F	,,
1741-2	,,	f	,,		1762-3	,,	G	,,
1742-3	,,	g	,,		†1763-4	,,	H	,,
1743-4	,,	h	,,		1764-5	,,	I	,,
1744-5	,,	i	,,		1765-6	,,	K	,,
1745-6	,,	k	,,		1766-7	,,	L	,,
1746-7	,,	l	,,		1767-8	,,	M	,,
1747-8	,,	m	,,		†1768-9	,,	N	,,
1748-9	,,	n	,,		1769-70	,,	O	,,
1749-50	,,	o	,,		1770-1	,,	P	,,
1750-1	,,	p	,,		†1771-2	,,	Q	,,
†1751-2		q			1772-3	,,	R	,,
1752-3	,,	r	,,		1773-4	,,	S	,,
1753-4	,,	r	,,		1774-5	,,	T	,,
1754-5	,,	t	,,		1775-6	,,	U	,,
1755-6	,,	u	,,					

* 1758-60   On articles bearing the hallmarks of 1758-9-60, the leopard's head crowned is occasionally found in a shield with pointed base.

† Date-letters for 1763-4, 1768-9, and 1771-2, are sometimes found to differ from those in general use thus:

1763-4 1768-9 1771-2

Year	LEOPARD'S HEAD CROWNED	DATE LETTER	LION PASSANT	KING'S HEAD
1776-7	☗	a	🦁	
1777-8	,,	b	,,	
1778-9	,,	c	,,	
1779-80	,,	d	,,	
1780-1	,,	e	,,	
1781-2	,,	f	,,	
1782-3	,,	g	,,	
1783-4	,,	h	,,	KING'S HEAD.
1784-5	,,	i	,,	👤
1785-6	,,	k	,,	,,
1786-7	,,	l	,,	👤
1787-8	,,	m	,,	,,
1788-9	,,	n	,,	,,
1789-90	,,	o	,,	,,
1790-1	,,	p	,,	,,
1791-2	,,	q	,,	,,
1792-3	,,	r	,,	,,
1793-4	,,	s	,,	,,
1794-5	,,	t	,,	,,
1795-6	,,	u	,,	,,

Year	LEOPARD'S HEAD CROWNED	DATE LETTER	LION PASSANT	KING'S HEAD
1796-7	☗	A	🦁	👤
1797-8	,,	B	,,	,,
1798-9	,,	C	,,	,,
1799 1800	,,	D	,,	,,
1800-1	,,	E	,,	,,
1801-2	,,	F	,,	,,
1802-3	,,	G	,,	,,
1803-4	,,	H	,,	,,
†1804-5	,,	I	,,	,,
1805-6	,,	K	,,	,,
1806-7	,,	L	,,	,,
1807-8	,,	M	,,	,,
1808-9	,,	N	,,	,,
1809-10	,,	O	,,	,,
1810-1	,,	P	,,	,,
1811-2	,,	Q	,,	,,
1812-3	,,	R	,,	,,
1813-4	,,	S	,,	,,
1814-5	,,	T	,,	,,
1815-6	,,	U	,,	,,

	LEOPARD'S HEAD	DATE LETTER.	LION PASSANT.	KING'S HEAD.
1816-7	🦁	a	🦁	👤
1817-8	,,	b	,,	,,
1818-9	,,	c	,,	,,
1819-20	,,	d	,,	,,
GEO. IV. 1820-1	,,	e	,,	👤
1821-2	🦁	f	🦁	,,
1822-3	,,	g	,,	,,
1823-4	,,	h	,,	,,
1824-5	,,	i	,,	,,
1825-6	,,	k	,,	,,
1826-7	,,	l	,,	,,
1827-8	,,	m	,,	,,
1828-9	,,	n	,,	,,
1829-30	,,	o	,,	,,
WM. IV. 1830-1	,,	p	,,	,,
1831-2	,,	q	,,	👤
1832-3	,,	r	,,	,,
1833-4	,,	s	,,	,,
1834-5	,,	t	,,	,,
1835-6	,,	u	,,	,,

YORK 1657-1832

	TOWN MARK	DATE LETTER
1657-8	●	A
1658-9	●	B
1659-60	●	C
1660-1	,,	D
1661-2	,,	E
1662-3	●	F
1663-4	●	G
1664-5	,,	H
1665-6	,,	I
1666-7	●	K
1667-8	,,	L
1668-9	,,	M
1669-70	,,	N
1670-1	●	O
1671-2	,,	P
1672-3	●	Q
1673-4	,,	R
1674-5	,,	S
1675-6	,,	T
1676-7	,,	U
1677-8	,,	V
1678-9	,,	W
1679-80	●	X
1680-1	,,	Y
1681-2	,,	Z

	TOWN MARK	DATE LETTER
1682-3	●	A
1683-4	,,	B
1684-5	●	C
JAS. II. 1685-6		D
1686-7	,,	E
1687-8	,,	F
1688-9	,,	G
WM. & MY. 1689-90		H
1690-1		I
1691-2	●	K
1692-3	,,	L
1693-4	,,	M
1694-5		N
1695-6	●	O
WM. III. 1696-7	,,	P
1697-8	,,	Q
1698-9	,,	R
1699 1700		S

	TOWN MARK	BRITANNIA	LION'S HEAD ERASED	DATE LETTER
1700-1	✠	●	●	A
1701-2	✠	●	●	B
ANNE. 1702-3	,,	,,	,,	C
1703-4	,,	,,	,,	D
1704-5				
1705-6	,,	,,	,,	F
1706-7	,,	,,	,,	G
1707-8				
1708-9	,,	,,	,,	I
1709-10				
1710-11				
1711-2	,,	,,	,,	m
1712-3				
1713-4	,,	,,	,,	o
GEO. I. 1714-5				
1715-6				
1716-7				

Very little, if any, plate was assayed and marked at York during th sixty years from 1716 to 1776.

	Town Mark.	Lion Passant.	Leopard's Head Crowned.	Date Letter.	King's Head.
1776-7				A	
1777-8				B	
1778-9				C	
1779-80		🦁	👑	D	
1780-1				E	
1781-2	🛡	,,	,,	F	
1782-3	,,	,,	,,	G	
1783-4	,,	,,	,,	H	
1784-5	,,	,,	,,	J	👤
1785-6				K	
1786-7				L	

	TOWN MARK.	LION PASSANT.	LEOPARD'S HEAD CROWNED	KING'S HEAD.	DATE LETTER.
1787-8	🛡	🦁	👑	👤	A
1788-9					b
1789-90	,,	,,	,,	,,	c
1790-1	,,	,,	,,	,,	d
1791-2	,,	,,	,,	,,	e
1792-3					f
1793-4	,,	,,	,,	,,	g
1794-5					h
1795-6	,,	,,	,,	,,	i
1796-7	,,	,,	,,	👤	k
1797-8					l or L
1798-9	,,	,,	,,	,,	M
1799 1800	,,	,,	,,	,,	N
1800-1	,,	,,	,,	,,	O
1801-2	,,	,,	,,	,,	P
1802-3	,,	,,	,,	,,	Q
1803-4	,,	,,	,,	,,	R
1804-5	,,	,,	,,	,,	S
1805-6	,,	,,	,,	,,	T
1806-7					U
1807-8	,,	,,	,,	,,	V
1808-9		,,	,,	,,	W
1809-10		,,	,,	,,	X
1810-1	,,	,,	,,	,,	Y
1811-2					Z

	TOWN MARK.	LION PASSANT.	LEOPARD'S HEAD CROWNED.	KING'S HEAD	DATE LETTER.
1812-3	✠	🦁	👑	👤	a
1813-4					b
1814-5					c
1815-6	,,	,,	,,	,,	d
1816-7					e
1817-8	,,	,,	,,	,,	f
1818-9	,,	,,	,,	,,	g
1819-20					h
GEO. IV. 1820-1		,,	,,	,,	i
1821-2		,,	,,	,,	k
1822-3					l
1823-4					m
1824-5	,,	,,	,,	,,	n
1825-6	,,	,,	,,	,,	o
1826-7		,,	,,	,,	p
1827-8					q
1828-9	,,	,,	,,	,,	r
1829-30	,,	,,	,,	,,	s
WM. IV. 1830-1	5	,,	,,	👤	t
1831-2		,,	,,	,,	u
1832-3					v
1833-4					w
1834-5					x
1835-6					y
1836-7					z

EXETER 1640-1698

DATE.	MARKS.
c. 1640-50	I·E 𝔄
,,	PR ✲ PR ✦
,,	✱ B
,,	✱ FA
,,	FA
c. 1646-98	X IF
c. 1670	X IAR
1676	✱
,,	✱
c. 1680	XON IV · X
,,	X
,,	,, IS
1690	M EX ON
c. 1690	✱ IS
,,	,, WE
,,	,, WE
,,	M ✱
,,	🦁 ✱ ⊛
,,	IP ✱ ✱ ✱
,,	X 🦁 IP
1694	EX NB ON
1698	♛X ✣ ✣ ✣

	CASTLE.	BRIT-ANNIA.	LION'S HEAD ERASED.	DATE LETTER
1701·2	⛫	🛡	🦁	**A**
ANNE. 1702·3	⛫	,,	,,	**B**
1703·4	⛫	,,	,,	**C**
1704·5	,,	,,	,,	**D**
1705·6	,,	,,	,,	**E**
1706·7	,,	,,	,,	**F**
1707·8	,,	,,	,,	**G**
1708·9	⛫	,,	,,	**H**
1709·10	⛫	,,	,,	**I**
1710·1	,,	,,	,,	**K**
1711·2	,,	,,	,,	**L**
1712·3	,,	,,	,,	**M**
1713·4	⛫	,,	,,	**N**
GEO. I. 1714·5	,,	,,	,,	**O**
1715·6	,,	,,	,,	**P**
1716·7	,,	,,	,,	**Q**
1717·8	,,	,,	,,	**R**
1718·9	,,	,,	,,	**S**
1719·20	,,	,,	,,	**T**
1720·1	,,	,,	,,	**V**
1721·2	⛫	🛡	🦁	**W**
1722·3				**X**
1723·4	,,	,,	,,	**Y**
1724·5	,,	,,	,,	**Z**

	CASTLE	LEOPARD'S HEAD CROWNED	LION PASSANT	DATE LETTER
1725-6	🏰	👑	🦁	**a**
1726-7	,,	,,	,,	**b**
GEO. II. 1727-8	,,	,,	,,	**c**
1728-9	,,	,,	,,	**d**
1729-30	,,	,,	,,	**e**
1730-1	,,	,,	,,	**f**
1731-2	,,	,,	,,	**g**
1732-3	,,	,,	,,	**h**
1733-4	,,	,,	,,	**i**
1734-5	,,	,,	,,	**k**
1735-6	,,	,,	,,	**l**
1736-7	,,	,,	,,	**m**
1737-8	,,	,,	,,	**n**
1738-9	,,	,,	,,	**o**
1739-40	,,	,,	,,	**p**
1740-1	,,	,,	,,	**q**
1741-2	,,	,,	,,	**r**
1742-3	,,	,,	,,	**s**
1743-4	,,	,,	,,	**t**
1744-5	,,	,,	,,	**u**
1745-6	,,	,,	,,	**w**
1746-7	,,	,,	,,	**x**
1747-8	,,	,,	,,	**y**
1748-9	,,	,,	,,	**z**

	CASTLE	LEOPARD'S HEAD CROWNED	LION PASSANT	DATE LETTER
1749-50	🏰	👑	🦁	**A**
1750-1	,,	,,	,,	**B**
1751-2	,,	,,	,,	**C**
1752-3	,,	,,	,,	**D**
1753-4	,,	,,	,,	**E**
1754-5	,,	,,	,,	**F**
1755-6	,,	,,	,,	**G**
1756-7	,,	,,	,,	**H**
1757-8	,,	,,	,,	**I**
1758-9	,,	,,	,,	**K**
1759-60	,,	,,	,,	**L**
GEO. III. 1760-1	,,	,,	,,	**M**
1761-2	,,	,,	,,	**N**
1762-3	,,	,,	,,	**O**
1763-4	,,	,,	,,	**P**
1764-5	,,	,,	,,	**Q**
1765-6	,,	,,	,,	**R**
1766-7	,,	,,	,,	**S**
1767-8	,,	,,	,,	**T**
1768-9	,,	,,	,,	**U**
1769-70	,,	,,	,,	**W**
1770-1	,,	,,	,,	**X**
1771-2	,,	,,	,,	**Y**
1772-3	,,	,,	,,	**Z**

	CASTLE	LEOPARD'S HEAD CROWNED	LION PASSANT	DATE LETTER
1773-4	🏰	👑	🦁	A
1774-5	,,	,,	,,	B
1775-6	,,	,,	,,	C
1776-7	,,	,,	,,	D
1777-8	,,	,,	,,	E
1778-9	,,		🦁	F
1779-80	,,	,,		G
1780-1	,,	,,		H
1781-2-3	,,			I
1783-4	,,	KING'S HEAD	,,	K
1784-5	,,	👤	,,	L
1785-6	,,	,,	,,	M
1786-7	,,	👤		N
1787-8	,,	,,	,,	O
1788-9	,,	,,	,,	P
1789-90	,,	,,	,,	q
1790-1	,,	,,	,,	r
1791-2	,,	,,	,,	f
1792-3	,,	,,	,,	t
1793-4	,,	,,	,,	u
1794-5	,,	,,	,,	w
1795-6	,,	,,	,,	x
1796-7	,,	,,	,,	y

	CASTLE	LION PASSANT	DATE LETTER	KING'S HEAD
1797-8	🏰	🦁	A	👤
1798-9	,,	,,	B	,,
1799 1800	,,	,,	C	👤
1800-1	,,	,,	D	,,
1801-2	,,	,,	E	,,
1802-3	,,	,,	F	,,
1803-4	,,	,,	G	,,
1804-5	,,	,,	H	,,
1805-6	🏰	🦁	I	,,
1806-7	,,	,,	K	,,
1807-8	,,	,,	L	,,
1808-9	,,	,,	M	,,
1809-10	,,	,,	N	,,
1810-1	,,	,,	O	,,
1811-2	,,	,,	P	,,
1812-3	,,	,,	Q	,,
1813-4	,,	,,	R	,,
1814-5	,,	,,	S	,,
1815-6	,,	,,	T	,,
1816-7	,,	,,	U	,,

	CASTLE.	LION PASSANT.	DATE LETTER.	KING'S HEAD.
1817-8	🏰	🦁	a	👤
1818-9	,,	,,	b	,,
1819-20	,,	,,	c	,,
GEO. IV. 1820-1	,,	,,	d	,,
1821-2	,,	,,	e	,,
1822-3	,,	,,	f	👤
1823-4	,,	,,	g	,,
1824-5	,,	,,	h	,,
1825-6	,,	,,	i	,,
1826-7	,,	,,	k	,,
1827-8	,,	,,	l	,,
1828-9	,,	,,	m	,,
1829-30	,,	,,	n	,,
WM. IV. 1830-1	,,	,,	o	,,
1831-2	🏰	🦁	p	👤
1832-3	,,	,,	q	,,
1833-4	🏰	🦁	r	,,
1834-5	,,	,,	s	👤
1835-6	,,	,,	t	,,
1836-7	,,	,,	u	,,

BIRMINGHAM 1773-1848

	LION PASSANT.	ANCHOR.	DATE LETTER.
1773-4	🦁	⚓	A
1774-5	,,	,,	B
1775-6	,,	,,	C
1776-7	,,	,,	D
1777-8	,,	,,	E
1778-9	,,	,,	F
1779-80	,,	,,	G
1780-1	,,	,,	H
1781-2	,,	,,	I
1782-3	,,	,,	K
1783-4	,,	,,	L

	LION PASSANT.	ANCHOR.	DATE LETTER.	KINGS HEAD
1784-5	,,	,,	M	👑
1785-6	,,	,,	N	,,
1786-7	,,	,,	O	👑
1787-8	,,	,,	P	,,
1788-9	,,	,,	Q	,,
1789-90	,,	,,	R	,,
1790-1	,,	,,	S	,,
1791-2	,,	,,	T	,,
1792-3	,,	,,	U	,,
1793-4	,,	,,	V	,,
1794-5	,,	,,	W	,,
1795-6	,,	,,	X	,,
1796-7	,,	,,	Y	,,
*1797-8	,,	,,	Z	👑

	LION PASSANT.	ANCHOR.	DATE LETTER.	KING'S HEAD
1798-9	🦁	⚓	a	👑
1799 / 1800	,,	,,	b	,,
1800-1	,,	,,	c	,,
1801-2	,,	,,	d	,,
1802-3	,,	,,	e	,,
1803-4	,,	,,	f	,,
1804-5	,,	,,	g	,,
1805-6	,,	,,	h	,,
1806-7	,,	,,	i	,,
1807-8	,,	,,	j	,,
1808-9	,,	,,	k	,,
1809-10	,,	,,	l	👑
1810-1	,,	,,	m	,,
1811-2	,,	,,	n	,,
1812-3	,,	,,	o	👑
1813-4	,,	,,	p	,,
1814-5	,,	,,	q	,,
1815-6	,,	,,	r	,,
1816-7	,,	,,	s	,,
1817-8	,,	,,	t	,,
1818-9	,,	,,	u	,,
1819-20 GEO. IV. / 1820-1	,,	,,	w	,,
1821-2	,,	,,	x	,,
1822-3	,,	,,	y	,,
1823-4	,,	,,	z	,,

SHEFFIELD 1773-1848

	LION PASSANT	CROWN	DATE LETTER	KING'S HEAD (from 1784)
1773-4	🦁	👑	E	
1774-5	,,	,,	F	
1775-6	,,	,,	N	
1776-7	,,	,,	R	
1777-8	,,	,,	H	
1778-9	,,	,,	S	
1779-80	,,	,,	A	
1780-1	,,	,,	T	
1781-2	,,	,,	D	
1782-3	,,	,,	G	
1783-4	,,	,,	B	
1784-5	,,	,,	I	●
1785-6	,,	,,	P	,,
1786-7	,,	👑	k	●
1787-8	,,	,,	C	,,
1788-9	,,	,,	M	,,
1789-90	,,	,,	Y	,,
1790-1	,,	,,	L	,,
1791-2	,,	,,	P	,,
1792-3	🦁	👑	U	,,
1793-4	,,	,,	O	,,
1794-5	,,	,,	m	,,
1795-6	,,	,,	q	,,
1796-7	,,	,,	Z	,,
1797-8	,,	,,	X	●
1798-9	,,	,,	V	●

	LION PASSANT	CROWN	DATE LETTER	KING'S HEAD
1799 1800	🦁	👑	E	●
1800-1	,,	,,	N	,,
1801-2	,,	,,	H	,,
1802-3	,,		M	,,
1803-4	,,	,,	F	,,
1804-5	,,	,,	G	,,
1805-6	,,	,,	B	,,
1806-7	,,	,,	A	,,
1807-8	,,	,,	S	,,
1808-9	,,	,,	P	,,
1809-10	,,	,,	K	,,
1810-1	,,		L	,,
1811-2	,,	,,	C	●
1812-3	,,	,,	D	,,
1813-4	,,	,,	R	,,
1814-5	,,		W	,,
1815-6	,,	,,	O	,,
1816-7	,,	,,	T	,,
1817-8	,,	,,	X	,,
1818-9	,,	,,	I	,,
1819-20	🦁	{ ,,	V	,,
			V	,,
GEO. IV. 1820-1	,,	,,	Q	,,
1821-2	,,	,,	Y	,,
1822-3	,,	,,	Z	,,
1823-4	,,	,,	U	,,

CHESTER 1668-1839

DATE.	MAKER'S MARK, TOWN MARK AND DATE-LETTER.
1668	
c. 1683	
,,	
c. 1685	
,,	
1686-90	
,,	
,,	
,,	
1690-2	
,,	
,,	
,,	
c. 1692	
1692-4	
1695-1700	
1695	
1696	
1697	

	BRITANNIA.	LION'S HEAD ERASED.	DATE LETTER.	TOWN MARK.
1701-2			A	
ANNE 1702-3	,,	,,	B	,,
1703-4	,,	,,	C	,,
1704-5	,,	,,	D	,,
1705-6	,,	,,	E	,,
1706-7	,,	,,	F	,,
1707-8	,,	,,	G	,,
1708-9	,,	,,	H	,,
1709-10	,,	,,	I	,,
1710-11	,,	,,	K	,,
1711-2	,,	,,	L	,,
1712-3	,,	,,	M	,,
1713-4 GEO. I. 1714-5	,,	,,	N	,,
	,,	,,	O	,,
1715-6	,,	,,	P	,,
1716-7	,,	,,	Q	,,
1717-8	,,	,,	R	,,
1718-9	,, LION PASSANT.	,, LEOP'S HEAD C?	S	,,
1719-20			T	.
1720-1	,,	,,	U	,,
1721-2	,,	,,	V	,,
1722-3	,,	,,	W	,,
1723-4	,,	,,	X	,,
1724-5	,,	,,	Y	,,
1725-6	,,	,,	Z	,,

	LION PASSANT	LEOPARD'S HEAD CROWNED	TOWN MARK	DATE LETTER
1726-7	🦁	👑	🛡	𝓐
GEO. II. 1727-8	,,	,,	,,	𝓑
1728-9	,,	,,	,,	𝓒
1729-30	,,	,,	,,	𝓓
1730-1	,,	,,	,,	𝓔
1731-2	,,	,,	,,	𝓕
1732-3	,,	,,	,,	𝓖
1733-4	,,	,,	,,	𝓗
1734-5	,,	,,	,,	𝓘
1735-6	,,	,,	,,	𝓚
1736-7	,,	,,	,,	𝓛
1737-8	,,	,,	,,	𝓜
1738-9	,,	,,	,,	𝓝
1739-40	,,	,,	,,	𝓞
1740-1	,,	,,	,,	𝓟
1741-2	,,	,,	,,	𝓠
1742-3	,,	,,	,,	𝓡
1743-4	,,	,,	,,	𝓢
1744-5	,,	,,	,,	𝓣
1745-6	,,	,,	,,	𝓤
1746-7	,,	,,	,,	𝓥
1747-8	,,	,,	,,	𝓦
1748-9	,,	👑	,,	𝓧
1749-50	,,	,,	,,	𝓨
1750-1	🦁	,,	,,	𝓩

	LION PASSANT	LEOPARD'S HEAD CROWNED	TOWN MARK	DATE LETTER
1751-2	🦁	👑	🛡	𝐚
1752-3	,,	,,	,,	B or b
1753-4	,,	,,	,,	C
1754-5	,,	,,	,,	D or d
1755-6	,,	,,	,,	e
1756-7	,,	,,	,,	F or f
1757-8	,,	,,	,,	G
1758-9	,,	,,	,,	h
1759-60	,,	,,	,,	I or i
GEO. III. 1760-1	,,	,,	,,	K or k
1761-2	,,	,,	,,	L or l
1762-3	,,	,,	,,	m
1763-4	,,	,,	,,	n
1764-5	,,	,,	,,	O
1765-6	,,	,,	,,	P
1766-7	,,	,,	,,	Q or q
1767-8	,,	,,	,,	R
1768-9	🦁	,,	,,	S
1769-70	,,	,,	,,	T
1771-2	,	,,	,,	U
1773	,,	,,	,,	V
1774	,,	,,	,,	W
1775	,,	,,	,,	X
1775-6	,,	,,	,,	Y

	LION PASSANT	LEOPARD'S HEAD CROWNED	TOWN MARK	DATE LETTER	KING'S HEAD
1776-7	🦁	👑	🛡	a	
1777-8	,,	,,	,,	b	
1778-9	,,	,,	,,	c	
1779-80	🦁	👑	🛡	d	
1780-1	,,	,,	,,	e	
1781-2	,,	,,	,,	f	
1782-3	,,	,,	,,	g	
1783-4	,,	,,	,,	h	
	,,	,,	,,		KING'S HEAD
1784-5 {	🦁	👑	🛡	i	👤
1785-6	,,	,,	,,	k	,,
1786-7	,,	,,	,,	l	👤
1787-8	,,	,,	,,	m	,,
1788-9	,,	,,	,,	n	,,
1789-90	,,	,,	,,	o	,,
1790-1	,,	,,	,,	p	,,
1791-2	,,	,,	,,	q	,,
1792-3	,,	,,	,,	r	,,
1793-4	,,	,,	,,	s	,,
1794-5	,,	,,	,,	t	,,
1795-6	,,	,,	,,	u	,,
1796-7	,,	,,	,,	v	,,

	LION PASSANT	LEOPARD'S HEAD CROWNED	TOWN MARK	DATE LETTER	KING'S HEAD
1797-8	🦁	👑	🛡	A	👤
1798-9	,,	,,	,,	B	,,
1799/1800	,,	,,	,,	C	,,
1800-1	,,	👑	,,	D	,,
1801-2	,,	,,	,,	E	,,
1802-3	,,	,,	,,	F	,,
1803-4	,,	,,	,,	G	,,
1804-5	,,	,,	,,	H	,,
1805-6	,,	,,	,,	I	,,
1806-7	,,	,,	,,	K	,,
1807-8	,,	,,	,,	L	,,
1808-9	,,	,,	,,	M	,,
1809-10	,,	,,	,,	N	,,
1810-1	,,	,,	,,	O	,,
1811-2	,,	,,	,,	P	,,
1812-3	,,	,,	,,	Q	,,
1813-4	,,	,,	,,	R	,,
1814-5	,,	,,	,,	S	,,
1815-6	,,	,,	,,	T	,,
1816-7	,,	,,	,,	U	,,
1817-8	,,	,,	,,	V	,,

	LION PASSANT.	LEOPARD'S HEAD.	TOWN MARK.	DATE LETTER.	KING'S HEAD.
1818-9	🦁	👑	👑	**A**	👤
1819-20	,,	,,	,,	**B**	,,
GEO. IV. 1820-1	,,	,,	,,	**C**	,,
1821-2-3	,,	,,	,,	**D**	,,
1823-4	,,	👑	,,	**E**	👤
1824-5	,,	,,	,,	**F**	,,
1825-6	,,	,,	,,	**G**	,,
1826-7	,,	,,	,,	**H**	,,
1827-8	,,	,,	,,	**I**	,,
1828-9	,,	,,	,,	**K**	,,
1829-30	,,	,,	,,	**L**	,,
WM. IV. 1830-1	,,	,,	,,	**M**	,,
1831-2	,,	,,	,,	**N**	,,
1832-3	,,	,,	,,	**O**	,,
1833-4	,,	,,	,,	**P**	,,
1834-5	,,	,,	,,	**Q**	,,
1835-6	,,	,,	,,	**R**	👤
1836-7	,,	,,	,,	**S**	,,
VICT. 1837-8	,,	,,	,,	**T**	,,
1838-9	,,	,,	,,	**U**	,,

NEWCASTLE 1658-1839

DATE (ABOUT).	MARKS.			
1658				
1664				
1668				
1670				
1672				
,,				
1675				
,,				
1680				
1684				
,,				
,,				
,,				
1685				
,,				
1686-7				
1686-8				
1690				
1692				
1694				
,,				
,,				
1695				
1697				
1698				
1698-9				
1700				
,,				
1701				

	THREE CASTLES.	BRIT ANNIA	LION'S HEAD ERASED.	DATE LETTER.
ANNE. 1702-3				
1703-4	,,	,,	,,	
1704-5	,,	,,	,,	
1705-6	,,	,,	,,	
1706-7	,,	,,	,,	
1707-8		,,	,,	
1708-9	,,	,,	,,	
1709-10	,,	,,	,,	,,
1710-11				
1711-2				
1712-3				
1713-4				
GEO. I. 1714-5		,,	,,	
1715-6				
1716-7				
1717-8	,,	,,	,,	
1718-9	,,	,,	,,	
1719-20	,,	,,	,,	
1720-1	,,	,,	,,	

,,   John Hewitt.   Tankard: Mr. G. Dunn.

	THREE CASTLES	LION PASSANT	LEOPARD'S HEAD CROWNED	DATE LETTER
1721-2	🛡	🦁	👑	A
1722-3	🛡	🦁	,,	B
1723-4	,,	🦁	,,	C
1724-5	,,	,,	,,	D
1725-6	🛡	🦁	👑	E
1726-7	,,	,,	,,	F
GEO. II. 1727-8	🛡	,,	👑	G
1728-9	,,	🦁	,,	H
1729-30	,,	,,	,,	I
1730-1	,,	,,	,,	K
1731-2	,,	,,	,,	L
1732-3	,,	,,	,,	M
1733-4	,,	,,	,,	N
1734-5	,,	,,	,,	O
1735-6	,,	,,	,,	P
1736-7	,,	,,	,,	Q
1737-8	,,	,,	,,	R
1738-9	,,	,,	,,	S
1739-40	,,	,,	,,	T

	THREE CASTLES	LION PASSANT	LEOPARD'S HEAD CROWNED	DATE LETTER
1740-1	🛡	🦁	👑	A
1741-2	,,	,,	,,	B
1742-3	,,	,,	,,	C
1743-4	,,	,,	,,	D
1744-5	,,	,,	,,	E
1745-6	,,	,,	👑	F
1746-7	🛡	🦁	👑	G
1747-8	,,	,,	,,	H
1748-9	,,	,,	,,	I
1749-50	,,	,,	,,	K
1750-1	,,	🦁	👑	L
1751-2	,,	,,	,,	M
1752-3	,,	,,	,,	N
1753-4	,,	,,	,,	O
1754-5	,,	,,	,,	P
1755-6	,,	,,	,,	Q
1756-7	,,	,,	,,	R
1757-8	🛡	,,	👑	S
1758-9				T

	THREE CASTLES	LION PASSANT	LEOPARD'S HEAD CROWNED	DATE LETTER	KING'S HEAD
1759-60	🏰	🦁	👑	A	
GEO. III. 1760-8	,,	,,	,,	B	
1769-70	,,	🦁	,,	C	
1770-1	🏰	,,	👑	D	
1771-2	,,	,,	,,	E	
1772-3	🏰	,,	,,	F	
1773-4	,,	,,	,,	G	
1774-5	,,	,,	,,	H	
1775-6	,,	,,	,,	I	
1776-7	,,	,,	,,	K	
1777-8	,,	,,	,,	L	
1778-9	,,	,,	,,	M	
1779-80	,,	🦁	👑	N	
1780-1	,,	,,	,,	O	
1781-2	,,	,,	,,	P	
1782-3	,,	,,	,,	Q	
1783-4	,,	,,	,,	R	
1784-5	,,	,,	,,	S	👤
1785-6	,,	,,	,,	T	,,
1786-7	,,	,,	,,	U	👤
1787-8	,,	🦁	👑	W	,,
1788-9	,,	🦁	,,	X	,,
1789-90	,,	,,	,,	Y	,,
1790-1	,,	,,	,,	Z	,,

	LION PASSANT	THREE CASTLES	LEOPARD'S HEAD CROWNED	KING'S HEAD	DATE LETTER
1791-2	🦁	🏰	👑	👤	A
1792-3	,,	,,	,,	,,	B
1793-4	,,	,,	,,	,,	C
1794-5	,,	,,	,,	,,	D
1795-6	,,	,,	,,	,,	E
1796-7	,,	,,	,,	,,	F
1797-8	,,	,,	,,	👤	G
1798-9	,,	,,	,,	,,	H
1799 1800	,,	,,	,,	,,	I
1800-1	🦁	🏰	👑	👤	K
1801-2	,,	,,	,,	,,	L
1802-3	,,	,,	,,	,,	M
1803-4	🦁	,,	,,	👤	N
1804-5	,,	,,	,,	,,	O
1805-6	,,	,,	,,	,,	P
1806-7	,,	,,	,,	,,	Q
1807-8	,,	,,	,,	,,	R
1808-9	,,	,,	,,	,,	S
1809-10	🦁	🏰	👑	👤	T
1810-1	,,	,,	,,	,,	U
1811-2	,,	,,	,,	,,	W
1812-3	,,	,,	,,	,,	X
1813-4	,,	,,	,,	,,	Y
1814-5	,,	,,	,,	,,	Z

	DATE LETTER	KING'S HEAD	LION PASSANT	THREE CASTLES	LEOPARD'S HEAD CROWNED
1815-6	A	◯	🦁	🏰	👑
1816-7	B	,,	,,	,,	,,
1817-8	C	,,	,,	,,	,,
1818-9	D	,,	,,	,,	,,
1819-20	E	,,	,,	,,	,,
GEO. IV. 1820-1	F	,,	,,	,,	,,
1821-2	G	◯	,,	,,	,,
1822-3	H	,,	,,	,,	,,
1823-4	I	,,	,,	,,	,,
1824-5	K	,,	,,	,,	,,
1825-6	L		,,	,,	,,
1826-7	M	,,	,,		,,
1827-8	N	,,	,,	,,	,,
1828-9	O	,,	,,	,,	,,
1829-30	P	,,	,,	,,	,,
WM. IV. 1830-1	Q	,,	,,	,,	,,
1831-2	R	,,	,,	,,	,,
1832-3	S	◯	,,	,,	,,
1833-4	T	,,	,,	,,	,,
1834-5	U	,,	,,	,,	,,
1835-6	W	,,	,,	,,	,,
1836-7	X	,,	,,	,,	,,
VICT. 1837-8	Y		,,	,,	,,
1838-9	Z	,,	,,	,,	,,

EDINBURGH 1681-1832

TOWN MARK. CASTLE.	ASSAY MASTER'S MARK.	DATE LETTER.	DATE.
🏰	B	𝔞	1681-2
,,	B	𝔟	1682-3
,,	,,	𝔠	1683-4
,,	,,	𝔡	1684-5
,,	,,	𝔢	1685-6
,,	,,	𝔣	1686-7
,,	,,	𝔤	1687-8
,,	,,	𝔥	1688-9 WM. & MY.
,,	,,	𝔦	1689-90
,,	,,	𝔨	1690-1
,,	,,	𝔩	1691-2
,,	,,	𝔪	1692-3
,,	,,	𝔫	1693-4
,,	,,	𝔬	1694-5 WM. III.
,,	,,	𝔭	1695-6
,,	P	𝔮	1696-7
,,	,,	𝔯	1697-8
🏰	,,	𝔰	1698-9
,,	,,	𝔱	1699 1700
,,	,,	𝔲	1700-1
,,	,,	𝔴	1701-2
,,	,,	𝔵	1702-3 ANNE.
,,	,,	𝔶	1703-4
,,	,,	𝔷	1704-5

TOWN MARK. CASTLE.	ASSAY MASTER'S MARK.	DATE LETTER.	DATE.
🏰	P	A	1705-6
,,	,,	B	1706-7
,,	EP	C	1707-8
,,	,,	D	1708-9
,,	,,	E	1709-10
,,	,,	F	1710-1
,,	,,	G	1711-2
,,	,,	H	1712-3
,,	,,	I	1713-4 GEO. I.
🏰	,,	K	1714-5
,,	,,	L	1715-6
,,	,,	MM	1716-7
,,	,,	NN	1717-8
🏰	EP	N	,,
,,	,,	O	1718-9
,,	,,	PP	1719-20
,,	EP	P	,,
,,	,,	q	1720-1
,,	,,	R	1721-2
,,	,,	S	1722-3
,,	,,	T	1723-4
,,	,,	U	1724-5
,,	,,	V	1725-6
,,	,,	W	1726-7 GEO. II.
,,	,,	X	1727-8
,,	,,	Y	1728-9
,,	AU	Z	1729-30

TOWN MARK CASTLE	ASSAY MASTER'S MARK	DATE LETTER	DATE.
🏰	AU	A	1730-1
,,	,,	B	1731-2
,,	,,	C	1732-3
,,	,,	D	1733-4
,,	,,	E	1734-5
,,	,,	F	1735-6
,,	,,	G	1736-7
🏰	,,	H	1737-8
,,	,,	I	1738-9
,,	,,	K	1739-40
,,	GED	L	1740-1
,,	,,	M	1741-2
,,	EL	N	1742-3
,,	,,	O	1743-4
🏰	HG	P	1744-5
,,	,,	Q	1745-6
,,	,,	R	1746-7
,,	,,	S	1747-8
,,	,,	T	1748-9
,,	,,	U	1749-50
,,	,,	V	1750-1
,,	,,	W	1751-2
,,	,,	X	1752-3
,,	,,	Y	1753-4
,,	,,	Z	1754-5

TOWN MARK CASTLE	ASSAY MASTER'S MARK	DATE LETTER	DATE.
🏰	HG	A	1755-6
,,	,,	B	1756-7
,,	,,	C	1757-8
,,	,, THISTLE	D	1758-9
,,	🌿	E	1759-60
,,	,,	F	GLO. III. 1760-1
,,	,,	G	1761-2
,,	,,	H	1762-3
,,	,,	I	1763-4
,,	,,	K	1764-5
,,	,,	L	1765-6
,,	,,	M	1766-7
,,	,,	N	1767-8
,,	,,	O	1768-9
,,	,,	P	1769-70
,,	,,	Q	1770-1
,,	,,	R	1771-2
,,	,,	S	1772-3
,,	,,	T	1773-4
,,	,,	U	1774-5
,,	,,	V	1775-6
,,	,,	X	1776-7
,,	,,	Y	1777-8
,,	,,	Z	1778-9
,,	,,	U	1779-80

TOWN MARK CASTLE	THISTLE	DATE LETTER	DATE.
🏰	🛡	**A**	1780-1
,,	,,	**B**	1781-2
,,	,,	**C**	1782-3
,,	,,	**D**	1783-4
KING'S HEAD 👤	,,	**E**	*1784-5
,,	,,	**F**	1785-6
👤	,,	**G**	†1786-7-8
,,	,,	**H**	1788-9
,,	,,	**IJ**	‡1789-90
,,	,,	**K**	1790-1
,,	,,	**L**	1791-2
,,	,,	**M**	1792-3
,,	,,	**N**	§1793-4
,,	,,	**O**	1794-5
,,	,,	**P**	1795-6
,,	,,	**Q**	1796-7
👤	,,	**R**	1797-8
,,	,,	**S**	1798-9
,,	🏰 🛡	**T**	1799 1800
,,	,,	**U**	1800-1
,,	,,	**V**	1801-2
,,	🏰	**W**	1802-3
,,	,,	**X**	1803-4
,,	,,	**Y**	1804-5
,,	,,	**Z**	1805-6

KING'S HEAD.	TOWN MARK CASTLE	THISTLE.	DATE LETTER	DATE.
👤	🏰	🛡	**a**	1806-7
,,	,,	,,	**b**	1807-8
,,	,,	,,	**c**	1808-9
,,	🏰	,,	**d**	1809-10
,,	,,	,,	**e**	1810-1
,,	,,	,,	**f**	1811-2
,,	,,	,,	**g**	1812-3
,,	,,	,,	**h**	1813-4
,,	,,	,,	**i**	1814-5
,,	,,	,,	**j**	1815-6
,,	,,	,,	**k**	1816-7
,,	,,	,,	**l**	1817-8
,,	,,	,,	**m**	1818-9
,,	,,	,,	**n**	1819-20
,,	🏰	🛡	**o**	GEO. IV 1820-1
,,	,,	,,	**p**	1821-2
,,	,,	,,	**q**	1822-3
👤	,,	,,	**r**	1823-4
,,	🏰	,,	**s**	1824-5
,,	,,	,,	**t**	1825-6
,,	🏰	,,	**u**	1826-7
,,	,,	,,	**v**	1827-8
,,	,,	,,	**w**	1828-9
,,	,,	,,	**x**	1829-30
,,	,,	,,	**y**	WM. IV. 1830-1
,,	,,	,,	**z**	1831-2

GLASGOW 1681-1845

DATE.	MAKER'S MARK.
1681-2	T·M
1682-3	B
1683-4	
1684-5	
1685-6	,,
1686-7	
1687-8	
1688-9	
1689-90	IS
1690-1	,,
1691-2	
1692-3	
1693-4	
1694-5	B
1695-6	
1696-7	B
1697-8	
1698-9	W.C
1699/1700	B
1700-1	IL
1701-2	IL
1702-3	
1703-4	
1704-5	{ TC / I·L }
1705-6	,,

DATE (ABOUT.)	MAKER'S MARK.
1706-7	
1707-8	IL
	,,
1709-10	W.C
1709-20	IF
,,	JL
1717-49	IB
1728-31	,,
1725-35	RL
1743-52	IG
,,	GLN
1747-60	ST
1756-76	DW
,,	
1757-80	IC
,,	JL
,,	J·S
1758-65	WN
,,	B&N

DATE (ABOUT).	MAKER'S MARK.
1763-70	AG
,,	,,
,,	,,
1773-80	IT
1776-80	M&C
,,	M&C
,,	RG
,,	RG
1783	T&H
,,	J·Mc
1777-90	WL
1782-92	JW
1785-95	ID
,,	,,
1781 1800	MF
1811-3	MF

	TREE, FISH & BELL.	LION RAMPANT.	DATE LETTER.	KING'S HEAD.
1819-20	🌳	🦁	A	👤
GEO. IV. 1820-1	🌳	,,	B	,,
1821-2	,,	,,	C	,,
1822-3	,,	,,	D	,,
1823-4	,,	,,	E	,,
1824-5	,,	,,	F	,,
1825-6	,,	,,	G	,,
1826-7	,,	,,	H	,,
1827-8	,,	,,	I	,,
1828-9	,,	,,	J	,,
1829-30	,,	,,	K	,,
WM. IV. 1830-1	,,	,,	L	,,
1831-2	,,	,,	M	,,
1832-3	,,	,,	N	👤
1833-4	,,	,,	O	,,
1834-5	,,	,,	P	,,
1835-6	,,	,,	Q	,,
1836-7	,,	,,	R	,,
VICT. 1837-8	,,	,,	S	,,
1838-9	,,	,,	T	,,
1839-40	,,	,,	U	,,
1840-1	,,	,,	V	,,
1841-2	,,	,,	W	,,
1842-3	,,	,,	X	,,
1843-4	,,	,,	Y	,,
1844-5	,,	,,	Z	,,

DUBLIN 1679-1846

	HARP CROWNED	DATE LETTER
1678-9		𝔄
1679-80	🜲	𝔅
1680-1	🜲	ℭ
1681-2	,,	𝔇
1682-3	,,	𝔈
1683-4		𝔉
JAS. II. 1685-6-7	,,	𝔊
1688 to 1692	🜲	ℌ 𝔍
WM. III. 1693-4-5	🜲	𝔎
1696-9	,,	𝔏

	HARP CROWNED	DATE LETTER
1699/1700	🜲	𝔐
1700-1	,,	𝔑
1701-2	🜲	𝔇
ANNE. 1702-3	🜲	𝔓
1703-4	,,	𝔔
1704-5-6	🜲	ℜ
1706-7-8	🜲	𝔖
1708-9-0	,,	𝔗
1710-1-2	🜲	𝔘
1712-3-4	🜲	𝔚
GEO I. 1714-5	,,	𝔜
1715-6	🜲	𝔜
1716-7		𝒵

	HARP CROWNED	DATE LETTER
1717-8	🛡	A
,,	🛡	,,
1718-9	,,	B
1719-20	🛡	C
,,	🛡	C
1720-1	🛡	A
1721-2	,,	B
1722-3	,,	C
1723-4	,,	D
1724-5	🛡	E
1725-6	,,	F
1726-7	,,	G
GEO. II. 1727-8	🛡	H
1728-9	,,	I
1729-30	🛡	K
1730-1	,,	L

	HARP CROWNED	DATE LETTER	HIBERNIA
1731-2	🛡	L	⬤
1732-3	,,	M	⬤
1733-4	,,	N	,,
1734-5	🛡	O	⬤
1735-6	,,	P	,,
1736-7	,,	Q	,,
1737-8	,,	R	,,
1738-9	,,	S	,,
1739-40	,,	T	,,
1740-1	,,	U	,,
1741-2-3	🛡	W	,,
1743-4	,,	X	,,
1745	,,	Y	,,
1746	,,	Z	,,

Year	HIBERNIA	DATE LETTER	HARP CROWNED
1747	☘	A	♛
1748	,,	B	,,
1749	,,	C	♛
1750	,,	D	,,
1751-2	,,	E E	♛
1752-3	,,	F	,,
1753-4	,,	G	,,
1754-5	,,	H	,,
1757	,,	I	,,
1758	,,	K	♛
1759	,,	L	,,
GEO. III. 1760	,,	M	,,
1761	,,	N	,,
1762	,,	O	♛
1763	,,	P	,,
1764	,,	Q	,,
1765	,,	R	,,
1766	,,	S	,,
1767	,,	T	♛
†1768	☘	U	,,
1769	☘	W	♛
1770	,,	X	,,
1771	,,	Y	♛
1772	,,	Z	,,

Year	HIBERNIA	DATE LETTER	HARP CROWNED
1773	☘	A	♛
1774	,,	B	,,
1775	,,	C	,,
1776	,,	D	♛
1777	,,	E	,,
1778	,,	F	,,
1779	,,	G	,,
1780	,,	H	,,
1781	,,	I	,,
1782	,,	K	,,
1783	,,	L	,,
1784	,,	M	,,
1785	,,	N	,,
1786	,,	O	,,
1787	☘	P	♛
1788	,,	Q	,,
1789	,,	R	,,
1790	,,	S	,,
1791	,,	T	,,
1792	,,	U	,,
1793	,,	W	,,
1794	☘	X	♛
1795	,,	Y	,,
1796	,,	Z	,,

 The Hibernia stamp of this form was used between 1752 and 1754, as well as the one of oval outline.

	HIBERNIA.	DATE LETTER.	HARP CROWNED.	KING'S HEAD.
1797	●	A	●	
1798	,,	B	,,	
1799	,,	C	,,	
1800	,,	D	,,	
1801	,,	E	,,	
1802	,,	F	,,	
1803	,,	G	,,	
1804	,,	H	,,	
1805	,,	I	,,	
1806	,,	K	,,	KING'S HEAD.
1807	,,	L	,,	●
1808	,,	M	,,	,,
1809	,,	N N	,,	●
1810	●	O O	●	,,
1811	,,	P	,,	,,
1812	,,	Q	,,	,,
1813	,,	R	,,	,,
1814	,,	S	,,	,,
1815	,,	T	,,	,,
1816	,,	U	,,	,,
1817	,,	W	,,	,,
1818	,,	X	,,	,,
1819	,,	Y	,,	,,
GEO. IV. 1820	,,	Z	,,	,,

	HIBERNIA.	DATE LETTER.	HARP CROWNED.	KING'S HEAD.
1821	●	A	●	●
1822	,,	B	,,	○
1823	,,	C	,,	,,
1824	,,	D	,,	,,
1825-6	,,	E e	,,	●
1826-7	,,	F	,,	○
1827-8	●	G	●	●
1828-9	●	H	●	●
1829-30	●	I	●	●
WM. IV. 1830-1	●	K	●	●
1831-2	●	L	●	●
1832-3	,,	M	,,	,,
1833-4	●	N	●	,,
1834-5	●	O	●	○
1835-6	,,	P	,,	,,
1836-7	,,	Q	,,	,,
VICT. 1837-8	,,	R	,,	,,
1838-9	,,	S	,,	●
1839-40	●	T	●	,,
1840-1	,,	U	,,	,,
1841-2	,,	V	,,	,,
1842-3	●	W	●	,,
1843-4	,,	X	,,	,,
1844-5	●	Y	●	,,
1845-6	●	Z	●	,,

CORK 1662-1838

DATE.	MARKS.
1662	IR
1663	
1670	WB WB
1673	IR IR IR
1679	RS RS
1680	SP SP
,,	W•B W•B
,,	
,,	IH IH IH
1691	IH IH IH
1683	RG RG RG
1686	RG
1690	,, RG ,, RG
1692	CW CW
,,	RG RG
1696	RG ,,
,,	WB ,,
,,	RG
,,	,, RG ,,
1697	CB CB
1700	RG
,,	AS
1705	RG RG
1709	WC

DATE.	MARKS.
1709	AB AB AB
1702-29	GB
1709	IW
1710	WC WC
,,	RG STERLING
1710-20	I·R STERLING
1712	RG
1715-25	RG STERLING
,,	,, IM
,,	WC STERLING WC
,,	WC ,, WC
1719	CR CR CR
,,	WC Sterling
1720	WC STERLING
,,	BB STERLING
,,	M·S STERLING
1720-30	TM STERLING
,,	W·N STERLING
,,	ED STERLING ED
1720-34	W.N
,,	WY
,,	E·I
1722	E·R

DATE.	MARKS.
1724	Tho·Lilly STERLING
1725-6	RM STERLING
1730	WN STERLING
,,	HN STERLING
1730-40	W·B STERLING
,,	IH STERLING IH
,,	CR STERLING CR
,,	STERLING I·H
,,	R·G
,,	CP CP CP
1720-37	W·MARTIN
,,	W·MARTIN
,,	W·M
,,	R*M
1730-40	WB STERLING WB
1731	T·BULL
1740	G·H STERLING
,,	G·H G·H
,,	WB WB
1740-50	RA
,,	AS STERLING
1745-70	STARLING G·H
,,	GH STERLING GH
,,	STARLING GH
,,	G*H GH GH G+H

DATE.	MARKS.
c. 1750	STERLING SB
1750-70	R·P STERLING
,,	II I·IRISH II
,,	H STERLING
1757-80	MD DERMOTT
,,	MD STER
,,	MD STERLING MD
,,	WR ,,
,,	WR ,,
,,	WR
,,	WR STERLING
,,	,, STERLING
,,	WR
,,	WR WR
,,	WR WR
,,	McD STERLING
,,	MD ,,
1760	L*R STARLING L*R
,,	IA STERLING IA
1760-80	WALSH SW STERLING
,,	C·B STERLING
,,	SW WALSH STERLING
,,	SW STERLING
,,	WALSH STERLING
,,	SW WALSH STERLING
,,	SW ,,
,,	SM ,,

DATE.	MARKS.
1760-80	STERLING
,,	DMC
,,	DMC STER
,,	STARLING C·B
,,	C·B DOLLAR
1760-85	IH STERLING
1765-95	CT ,, CT
1770	IRH STD
,,	TA STERLING TA
,,	McD Sterling
,,	MD STERLING
1770-88	STER / JMS / STER
1770-99	IN STERLING
,,	IN STERLING
,,	IN ,,
,,	,, NICOLSON
1777 / 1820	PW STERLING
1780	C·T STERLING
,,	IH STERLING IH
,,	I·H ,,
,,	JH STERLING
,,	I·H STERLING
,,	CT STERLING
,,	SC STERLING
,,	S·R ,,
,,	JJX ,,
,,	TC STIRLING

DATE.	MARKS.
1770-80	W·M STERG
1770-99	NICOLSON STERLING
1777 / 1810	S·R STERLING
,,	S·R STERLING
,,	SR STERLG
,,	REILY STERLING
1783-95	W·ROE STERLING
,,	TG STERLING TG
1786-95	TH STERLING
1787-95	TC STERLG TC
1787	TD STERLING
1787-95	JS ,,
,,	IG STERLING
1787-99	R·S STERLING
,,	R-S STERLING
,,	I·S ,, I·S
,,	STERLING SHEEHAN
,,	SHEEHAN STERG
,,	SHEEHAN STERLING
,,	R·S STERLING
1790 / 1800	JMcN STERLING
,,	RI STERLING
1795	WT STERLG
,,	W·T STERLING
,,	WT STERLING
,,	,, STERLG

DATE	MARKS
1795	S
,,	WT (crown) STERLING
,,	WT STERLING
,,	HSM STERLING
,,	WT ,,
,,	TJB STERLING
1791	IW ,,
1780-99	,, STIRLING
1795	IW STERLING
,,	I·W STER
,,	I·W STERLING
,,	I·W STERLG
,,	STERLING / TOLLAND / STERLING
1796	I·H STERLING
,,	RD STERLING
,,	HEYLAND (crown) STERLING
,,	JK STERLING
,,	JMd
1800	IT TOLEKEN
,,	TWM STERLING
1800-20	GIBSON / STERLING / GIBSON
,,	WHELPLEY STERLING
,,	,, WHELPLY
,,	H ,, WHELPLY

DATE	MARKS
1800-20	GIBSON STERLING
,,	HEYLAND ,,
,,	,, TOLEKEN
1795 / 1807	T&W ,,
1805	SG STIRLING
1805-14	SG / STERLING / SG
,,	C·T / I·W STERLING
,,	T.MONTJOY ,,
,,	IN / NN ,,
1807-21	CT / IW STERLING
1808-20	·CORBETT· STERLING
1809-30	JS STERLING
,,	R·G ,,
1810	T·MONTJOY STERLING
,,	CONWAY / STERLING
,,	IE STERLING
,,	P.W STERLING
1810-20	WS STERLING
,,	I SOLOMON STERLING
,,	IS STERLING
,,	I·SOLOMON ,,
,,	FS ,,
,,	PG STERLING
1810-40	IS ,,
1812	GARDE STERLING
1820	SEYMOUR STERLING
1820-40	KM ,,
,,	EH ,,
1824	O BRIEN STERLING
,,	MAHONY / STERLING
1838	M&B STERLING